GUIDELINES FOR CONTEMPORARY CATHOLICS

The Eucharist

GUIDELINES FOR CONTEMPORARY CATHOLICS

THE EUCHARIST

Mary G. Durkin

THE THOMAS MORE PRESS
Chicago, Illinois

Copyright © 1990 by Mary Durkin. All rights reserved. Printed in the United States of America. No part of this publication may be reproduced, stored in a retrieval system, or transmitted, in any form or by any means, electronic, mechanical, photocopying, recording, or otherwise, without the written permission of the publisher, The Thomas More Association, 205 W. Monroe St., Chicago, IL 60606.

ISBN 0-88347-244-9

CONTENTS

INTRODUCTION
9

PART ONE
The Eucharist: A Sacrament

CHAPTER ONE
Religious Symbols
17

CHAPTER TWO
The Catholic Sacraments
29

PART TWO
The History

CHAPTER THREE
The Eucharist: Its Beginnings
59

CHAPTER FOUR
From Fellowship Meal to Private Worship
82

PART THREE
The Eucharist in the Modern World

CHAPTER FIVE
From Silent Mass to Eucharistic Celebration
117

CHAPTER SIX
Post-Vatican II
132

CHAPTER SEVEN
The Eucharist: 2013
155

READING LIST
169

QUESTIONS FOR DISCUSSION
173

For

The Montagues

Julie, Wayne & Andrew Alexander

INTRODUCTION

Do this in remembrance of me.
                                        Luke 22:20

Fundamentally the Eucharist is a victory—a victory of one who is absent to become present in a world which conceals him.
                                        St. Cyril of Alexandria

WHEN contemporary Catholics celebrate the Eucharist, they remember. They experience the Eucharist and its call to action in the immediate present. By their remembering, however, they are drawn into communion with all who have celebrated Jesus' victory for the last 2000 years. Their contemporary experience of the Eucharist can be deepened if they understand how the tradition of the past is continually reappropriated by the present.

It is essential that those searching for a mature grasp of the Catholic faith try to understand and appreciate the central mystery of the Eucharist. While this book was in preparation, an event took place which illustrates how important this mystery is to any contemporary discussion of Catholicism.

In June of 1988, Archbishop Marcel Lefebvre received

Mary G. Durkin

worldwide attention when he ordained four bishops. These new bishops are themselves empowered to ordain priests. Lefebvre's act ensured that his opposition to the reforms of the Second Vatican Council would continue after his death. Lefebvre and his followers argue, among other points, that the liturgical reforms of the Council attack essential truths of the Catholic faith.

The media covered Lefebvre's defiant act by showing members of his Society of St. Pius X attending a Tridentine Mass. Latin liturgy makes a good sound-bite. By focusing on the retention of Latin in this Mass, however, the media overlook a critical issue. Of far deeper significance is Lefebvre's adherence to an Order of the Mass issued by Pius V in 1570. Lefebvre believes that "the *sacrifice* of the Mass is the heart, the soul and the mystical wellspring of the Church." (Italics added.) For him, the Mass sums up the Catholic faith and, at the same time, continues the sacrifice of the Cross. He sees Vatican II's revision of the "Order of the Mass" as a challenge to the heart and soul of the faith. Lefebvre therefore opposes references to "the Eucharistic meal."

His problems with Vatican II go beyond liturgical reform, however. He refused to sign *The Pastoral Constitution on the Church in the Modern World* and *The Declaration on Religious Liberty*. He also disapproves of ecumenism. He finds the Church too influenced by liberalizing, Protestant forces. The movement towards a new understanding of the Eucharist threatens his concept of the Catholic Church.

Contemporary Catholics under the age of thirty might

The Eucharist

well wonder why anyone would consider it offensive to call the Mass a eucharistic meal. To them, the words *Eucharist* and *Mass* seem synonymous. As it is, they shake their heads when they hear their parents talk about growing up Catholic. Often, the younger folks cannot believe that people actually did the things Catholics did in those days.

The rituals of the pre-Vatican II Mass seem far removed from life and faith in the modern world. The Latin Mass is but one of many practices younger Catholics find strange. They cannot understand how their elders could have been so unquestioning about their faith and about religious practices.

Older Catholics react differently. They recall pre-Vatican II days when Eucharist and Mass were not synonymous. They attended Mass and sometimes received communion. Holy Eucharist was one of the seven sacraments. They received this sacrament for the first time when they made their First Holy Communion. Like Penance, but unlike the other sacraments, communion could be received more than once. Catholics received communion after the priest consecrated the bread and wine, turning it into the body and blood of Christ. Latin as the language of the Mass was a sign of the unity of the Church throughout the world. All Catholics followed the same ritual.

They thought that Catholics had always followed these practices and would continue to worship this way until the end of time. Moreover, if they studied the Catholic faith, they found presentations of a similar separation of Mass and Eucharist. They learned about a theology of the Mass

Mary G. Durkin

and a theology of the Real Presence. They probably found the Eucharist treated under a separate theology of sacraments.

While some older Catholics wax nostalgically about the solemnity of the old Mass, statistics show that the majority approve of the liturgical reform. Even when a Sunday liturgy is mediocre, regular churchgoers do not long for a return to an earlier era. At the very least, the reforms make it possible for them to participate in worship more than in the past.

Often, neither the younger nor the older Catholic reflects on the different visions of Church and faith represented by these two understandings of the Eucharist. Lefebvre is correct. The act of worship by which Catholics celebrate the continuing presence of Christ in their midst sums up the faith of the community. Yet he rejects the notion that the liturgical reforms help that faith come alive for Catholics in the modern world.

A contemporary understanding of the Eucharist requires an investigation of the Vatican Council's position on the Eucharist. The Council regarded the Eucharist as the basic expression of the Christian community. This position demanded a reform of the liturgy. Without this reform, the Council could not begin to turn toward its goal of making Christ present in the modern world. Good liturgical worship calls attention to this goal.

Many theological and liturgical issues grow out of this new focus on the Eucharist. Most people who participate in Sunday liturgies pay little attention to discussions of these issues. They are no more interested in arguments

The Eucharist

about memorial meal and thanksgiving than their ancestors were about transubstantiation and sacrifice.

Still, some background knowledge helps contemporary Catholics grasp the rationale behind the Church's concerns about eucharistic worship. This knowledge will also help Catholics evaluate how the Eucharist both expresses and challenges the heart of their Christian community.

As a sacrament, the Eucharist is both an object and an action. The definition of a sacrament found in the *Baltimore Catechism* needs updating in light of new insights into the role of religion in human experience. Scientific studies in anthropology reveal that religion plays a role in all human cultures. Those who study the history of religions find evidence of similar rituals in different faiths. New insights into Christology and ecclesiology provide a deeper appreciation of the meaning of the Catholic sacraments. Chapter One takes an overall look at how sacraments function as religious symbols. Chapter Two reviews the history of the Catholic sacramental system. An understanding of sacraments provides the framework for any inquiry into the meaning of the Eucharist, the core Catholic sacrament.

Some scholars apply scientific methods to their study of the written heritage of the Jewish and Catholic religions. The results of their study enhance any study of the Eucharist. The Bible, after all, contains the first accounts of Jesus' command to remember him. Chapter Three examines what biblical research reveals about the significance of Jesus' action at the Last Supper. It also examines the response of the early Christian community to his directive.

Mary G. Durkin

Historical research has helped to trace the evolution of the Mass to the present day. Historical data also provide information about the roots of various ongoing theological discussions associated with the Eucharist. For Catholics, Tradition (with a capital T), as well as the Bible, proves the validity of certain beliefs, while tradition (with a small t) appears in the religious imagination of the faithful. It, too, offers insights into how the Eucharist helped or hindered the making present of Jesus in the world. Chapter Four traces the history of the liturgical practices and theological discussions associated with the Eucharist.

When the Second Vatican Council initiated liturgical changes, it was responding to the findings of biblical and historical research and to the needs of the modern world. These changes were greater than any which had occurred in the previous four centuries. Chapter Five examines how new eucharistic ideas emerged from the Council.

The changes the Council set in motion were so sweeping that they altered the Catholic Church in a way Council participants never imagined. Liturgical changes were designed to make the challenge of faith more evident in the modern world. But the changes also raised questions about the meaning of that faith. Theologians and liturgists began studying the meaning of the Eucharist as a sacramental object and a sacramental action. In addition, ecumenism led to discussions about similarities and differences in eucharistic theology among the various Christian churches.

These questions elicited numerous post-conciliar papal statements about the Eucharist and directives on it from various Vatican congregations. Many of these pronounce-

The Eucharist

ments seek to correct what the *magisterium* sees as abuses. Others outline what Church authorities consider to be proper liturgical practices. The ecumenical dialogue on the Eucharist following the Council also demands the *magisterium's* position on the Eucharist be clarified. Chapter Six analyzes the *magisterium's* response to theological, liturgical, and ecumenical issues that were raised in discussions about the Eucharist.

Finally, the Church has implemented liturgical reforms unevenly. The inevitable tension resulting from a period of upheaval has both positive and negative effects. Yet it is still possible for a Eucharist to celebrate the victory of the absent/present one. Chapter Seven, building on the new understanding of the Eucharist outlined in the previous chapters, looks ahead and suggests how the Eucharist might develop as the Church enters the twenty-first century.

Contemporary Catholics who see the Eucharist as expressing the basis of their faith benefit from this broad approach to a study of the Eucharist in three ways. First, they learn about the rich history of the core sacrament of the Church. Second, they see how the victory of the one made present in the Eucharist challenges them to action in the modern world. Finally, they gain insights that can fuel their religious imagination, making it more responsive to the mystery that occurs in every eucharistic celebration.

PART ONE

THE EUCHARIST: A SACRAMENT

A sacrament is an outward sign instituted by Christ to give grace.

The Baltimore Catechism

A sacrament is a prophetic symbol, established by and modeled upon Christ the symbol of God, in and by which the Church, the Body of Christ, proclaims, realizes and celebrates for believers who place no obstacles that presence and action of God, which is rightly called grace.

Michael G. Lawler
Symbol and Sacrament, 1987

CHAPTER ONE

Religious Symbols

THE Catholic understanding of sacraments is quite different in the 1980s from what it was at the time *The Baltimore Catechism* appeared. Michael Lawler's definition, while

Mary G. Durkin

not contradicting that of the catechism, expands the meaning of each word beyond its original intent.

In this, he is in agreement with the sacramental theologians of the day. They call upon the insights of various disciplines within theology *and* the investigations of human experience by anthropologists and others studying human sciences. As a result, today's sacramental theologians are developing an increased appreciation for the rich sacramental tradition of the Church.

This contemporary study of the Eucharist, the core of the Catholic sacramental system, begins by reviewing current thinking about religious symbols. From their different perspectives, the human sciences, biblical research, Church history, and current theological and liturgical discussions all contribute to a contemporary understanding of the Eucharist.

The Human Sciences

One important difference between *The Baltimore Catechism* and most present-day understandings of sacraments is that the present-day emphasizes experience. Contemporary sacramental theology recognizes that sacraments grow out of and speak to human experience. Liturgical reforms seek to correlate experience and faith. People attending sacramental liturgies are no longer simply passive observers, waiting for the moment when grace will be poured into their souls. Instead, they are active participants whose experiences help shape the ritual.

The Eucharist

This new emphasis on experience is the result of knowledge gained from the scientific study of human behavior and development. Research by psychologists, sociologists, historians, and anthropologists, as well as new insights from philosophers, support the idea that there is a basic human need for sacramental experiences. This research also underscores the need to relate sacraments to experience.

Investigations into the way humans communicate show how important signs and symbols are to the human search for order and meaning. Anthropologists studying human cultures have also identified various systems humans create in their search for meaning. Their research supports the claim that sacraments—religious symbols imbedded into a system—have meaning even in a modern, secular culture.

Sign and Symbol

What is the difference between an "outward sign" and a "prophetic symbol"? Perhaps not as much as might seem at first glance. A prophetic symbol certainly qualifies as an outward sign. It is also possible to read more into "sign" and thus make it appear similar to "symbol." Yet the study of human patterns of communication shows that a symbol can imply much more than a sign. The concept of sacrament as symbol expresses a richer understanding of sacramental possibilities than the concept of sacrament as sign.

Humans are meaning-creating animals. The archaeolo-

Mary G. Durkin

gist Richard Leakey observes that humans, conceived in an animal culture, came to maturity in self-generating cultures. In these self-generating cultures, humans create meaning. When they come upon an object, they ask two questions: What is it? and What does it mean? So, too, with their experiences: they want to know what is happening and what is its meaning.

The ability to ascribe meaning to objects and experiences appears to be unique to human culture. Humans share with other life forms basic instincts for physical survival. That which distinguishes them as human, however, emerges when they try to attach meaning to experience.

As meaning-creating animals, humans are also symbol-making. They interpret their experiences through symbols. They communicate with each other through symbols. They use these symbols to create meaning. Within human cultures, both signs and symbols communicate meaning. All symbols can be regarded as signs, but all signs are not symbols. Moreover, humans cannot communicate by signs alone. They need symbols.

A sign points to a known entity. The meaning of the sign comes from either human agreement or convention. A stop sign is a conventional means of telling a driver to halt. A sign is transparent. It has only one meaning. Drivers readily recognize a stop sign and know that it does not mean "go" or "slow down." It means "halt." A sign also appeals to the intellect as it communicates abstract, objective meaning. A stop sign might elicit frustration, but that emotion is unrelated to the meaning of the sign. Its mean-

The Eucharist

ing is objective: the driver must halt. In addition, signs announce what they signify but do not cause the result. The stop sign does not cause the busy intersection but merely tells the driver to halt at it.

A sign becomes a symbol when it has meaning beyond that which it signifies and when the human who encounters it recognizes it as a symbol. A chair signifies something to sit upon. A chair usually has no other meaning. People will agree on what a chair is and on its meaning without recourse to subjective interpretations.

However, what if a chair was the only piece of new furniture purchased by newlyweds fifty years ago and the favorite chair of a husband, always placed in a special corner in each new residence? That chair then becomes symbolic of the husband and of the marriage. When his widow must rid herself of furniture in her move from their big house to a small apartment, the chair might be the only piece she insists on keeping, perhaps over the objections of her children.

A symbol differs from a mere sign in its living, subjective meaning. For the husband, the chair symbolized his special place in the house. For the widow, the chair represents the excitement of struggling newlyweds making their first purchase, fifty years of marriage with its ups and downs, and the presence of a husband. In her move, it means a link with her past. Perhaps at some point in the future, one of her children will view the chair as a link to the family's past. A symbol is opaque: it has many meanings.

Mary G. Durkin

Symbols also speak to the imagination. The widow's children may look upon the chair as an old piece of furniture, out of place in their mother's new apartment. It doesn't spark the same images in their imaginations as it does in hers. Because symbols are linked with the imagination, they are richer in meaning and power than signs. A symbol grabs the whole person. The chair makes the widow's life with her husband real to her in a way that reassures her when she is lonely or depressed. His presence, through the chair, encourages her to hope that life still has meaning.

Symbols make concretely present what they symbolize. The symbol expresses a reality that is not present, thereby seeming to make it present. The symbol represents that reality, is that reality for those who experience it, but is not the whole reality. A flag stands for a country but is not the whole meaning of that country. So, too, for the widow, the chair makes her husband present to her, but the chair does not convey all that her husband was or is.

Both objects and actions can be symbols. A country's flag reminds people of what the country stands for. The ceremonies during which the flag is displayed further serve to enhance this symbol. Draping the flag on the coffin of a war veteran, folding it, and giving it to the family at the grave site link the heroic action of the veteran to pride in one's country. The ceremonial actions associated with the flag are rituals. Rituals, be they those of a family, a school, a church, or a country, are symbolic actions.

There are both private and public symbols, and public symbols can have both public and private meaning. The

The Eucharist

chair is a private symbol, having meaning for the widow and perhaps for her and her husband during his lifetime. Their marriage was a public symbol. The communities to which married couples belong—church, state, family—dictate certain behaviors that order human relationships, including marriage.

Community members view marriage as a way of achieving the goals of the particular community. Though the different communities to which one belongs might interpret the meaning of marriage differently, they generally agree that marriage is a public symbol.

Public symbols acquire their meaning from the community that creates the symbol. For a flag to be a symbol, members of a nation must agree on the meaning of their flag. In addition, many persons understand and participate in a public symbol to the degree that they are members of the community. The symbol of the American flag has many different meanings for an American yet might have no meaning for someone from another country. For the latter, the American flag might remain simply a sign.

In general, this analysis of symbols reveals that humans depend on symbolic thinking and action for their existence. Those who would dismiss the importance of either an object or an action because it is "only a symbol" fail to appreciate how unique and necessary symbol-making is to humankind.

Sacraments, both objects and actions, function as public symbols. The Eucharist as bread and wine and the Eucharist as the ritual associated with that bread and wine are

Mary G. Durkin

public religious symbols. The meaning of these symbols is that which the religious community assigns to them.

Religious Symbols

In discussions of religious symbols, the question often arises about the relevance of sacraments in a modern, scientific and technological world. Previous cultures formulated religious answers in response to questions of meaning. Some people claim these religious answers no longer seem necessary. Individuals and societies rarely bother to search for meaning beyond that which is answered by science and technology. When humans walk on the moon, and an egg and a sperm join in a petri dish, it seems that science has now or will soon have the answer to all life's mysteries.

The "God is dead" cry of some theologians in the 1960s arose from their view of human experience. To them, it seemed that all the meaningful questions were answered. While they did not reject the power of symbols, they believed that secular symbols satisfied the human search for meaning.

Those theologians of the 60s neglected to apply to their own theological thinking the scientific method that they claimed made religion obsolete. They based their assumptions about human experience on their perceptions of that experience. They ignored the scientific study of human experience which was taking place within the social sciences. If they had used these findings about human experience,

The Eucharist

they would have discovered a different picture of the human search for meaning.

The cultural anthropologist Clifford Geertz identifies three meaning systems which all human cultures use to order life. His typology reveals that even in a scientific, technological, secular world, humans need religious symbols.

The first system, the common-sense meaning system, guides much human activity. At this level of meaning, humans respond unconsciously to the need for order in their lives. They use patterns of behavior acquired over the years. A person's daily rituals—from getting out of bed, to taking the train to work, to preparing meals, to retiring at the end of the day—are replete with examples of how common sense works.

Common sense helps humans make order out of what would otherwise be chaos. It aids a species that does not possess instinctive knowledge of how to create such order. People seldom experience mystery in this common-sense area of life. However, without common sense to explain why things are the way they are or what an individual should do in a certain situation, simple tasks would be a constant challenge.

Second, there is a scientific meaning system. This system addresses many of those questions that are not satisfied by common-sense answers. At this level, people begin to "figure out" answers to various problems. They observe that repeated actions produce similar results, and they draw conclusions based on cause and effect. For primitive humans, this scientific meaning system led to the discovery of

Mary G. Durkin

various uses for fire. For moderns, it meant putting people on the moon.

Scientific thinking is the hallmark of contemporary society. It answers many of the questions earlier societies had about the meaning of their experiences. Consequently, many humans experience less of a sense of mystery in their lives. Even if individuals do not personally know the answer to a question, they assume some scientific answer is available—or will be available soon.

The inability of the scientific meaning system to answer every question humans ask creates a third meaning system. This system functions when people face questions of ultimate meaning. Geertz labels this the religious (with a small "r") meaning system.

The ultimate questions deal with issues of life, death, immortality, good, and evil. How does life begin? What happens when I die? Is this world all there is to life or will I survive after death? Why are there good and evil in the world? All cultures, past and present, seek answers to these questions. The answers come from whatever it is that an individual or a society believes to be the ultimate meaning of life. The answers also affect the values and behaviors of the members of the community.

The answers of the religious meaning system are not scientifically verifiable in the same way a mathematical equation is. Still, they are necessary for ordering human experience. Human communities rely on symbols to express their answers to these ultimate questions. Individuals accept these answers to the degree that they participate in a partic-

The Eucharist

ular religious community (including the one that accepts secular answers to ultimate questions).

While all religious communities do not include a sacramental system as elaborate as that of the Catholic Church, all use symbolic objects and actions when confronting ultimate questions. When faced with the unexplainable mysteries of human experience, symbols offer the only possible answers. These answers are no less *real* than scientifically verifiable answers. They function, however, in a different, symbolic way. They appeal to the whole person. They speak to the imagination, while not ignoring the intellect. Although other religious communities may not call these symbols sacraments, their rituals are still what St. Augustine would call "signs of sacred reality."

The ritual system of any religion uses objects, places, actions, and people to address questions of meaning. These systems take experiences of human life and assign meaning to them through symbolic objects and actions. The religious community assigns a meaning to an experience which links it to the community's idea of ultimate meaning. The experiences chosen usually relate to ultimate questions.

People confront questions of ultimate meaning during times of birth, maturation, sex, sharing meals, building and disruption of the community, and death. Other religions besides Catholicism interpret these moments as times when their god is present to human experience. Even secular communities that reject the notion of god have symbolic rituals associated with these moments. Thus initiation rites, rites of passage, marriage rites, ordination rites,

Mary G. Durkin

ritual meals, rites of sacrifice and atonement, and funeral rites are among the many symbolic actions studied by history of religion scholars.

Combined research in the human sciences and the history of religion shows that objects and actions of sacred rituals are part of the meaning-making, symbol-creating power of humans. These symbolic actions, including the Catholic sacraments, are valid ways for people to enter into the meanings expressed by the rituals. Sacraments give people the opportunity to reaffirm these meanings. They also increase the participants' understanding of the meaning.

CHAPTER TWO

The Catholic Sacraments

THE Catholic sacramental system expresses meaning through symbols. The definition of sacraments in *The Baltimore Catechism* implies that each of the seven sacraments was instituted by Jesus. Yet there is no historical evidence that Jesus laid out the specific sacramental system that developed in the Church. Still, the Church maintains that both the Bible and Tradition affirm the validity of its sacramental practices. Since the Eucharist is the core sacrament of the Catholic system, it is helpful to review how that system developed.

When new historical and literary methods are applied to studies of the Bible and Tradition, the phrase "instituted by Christ" acquires a new meaning. While Jesus did not specify the sacramental system that came into being, his sacramental imagination attested to the potential religious symbolism of human experiences. His followers at a later time incorporated his message into a faith perspective that led to a unique sacramental system.

Mary G. Durkin
Biblical Studies

The New Testament tells how Jesus performed and participated in rituals with his followers, often giving new meaning to the actions. When his followers practiced these rituals, they felt that they brought the Lord into their midst. The present Catholic sacramental system with its seven sacraments grew out of a Catholic interpretation of these biblical practices as well as out of an understanding of what Jesus meant by his teachings.

Old Testament Roots

Neither Jesus nor his message developed in a vacuum. Jesus was a Jew. The rituals in which he engaged were rituals of the Jewish tradition. His original followers were Jews who initially saw no need to break with their Jewish roots. As a result, Jewish notions about ritual undoubtedly played a role in the early development of Christian sacraments.

The ancient Israelite community found their God in their history. For them, Yahweh lived and acted in human history. He was not like the nature gods that were honored by other people.

In *Clothed in Christ,* Michael Downey describes the world of the Israelites' contemporaries as *sacralized.* The sun, moon, and stars were gods. Animate and inanimate creation had magical power. Stones, plants, animals, trees, and other objects were sacred. Man-made statues could

The Eucharist

evoke the power of the gods. In their rituals these nature worshipers relied heavily on magic.

This approach was anathema to the Israelites. They communicated with Yahweh, not through ritual magic, but through remembrance of their sacred history. For this reason, some scholars look upon the Israelites' history as their most important sacrament. The scriptures that told the history were the second most important sacrament.

Yahweh guided and directed his people from the promise to Abraham, through the escape from Egypt and the wandering in the desert, to the covenant on Sinai, and the eventual conquest of Canaan. After they settled in the Promised Land and even when their nation was overcome, he was in their midst. Yahweh intervened in their world, and each time they retold their story, they came to a renewed sense of its meaning.

During their yearly remembrance of historical events, the Israelites recalled Yahweh's plan for his people. At the same time, they reflected on the meaning of these events and on the world view that grew out of them. This view is expressed in a variety of ways in the Old Testament writings.

Their view of a largely *desacralized* world in which the Israelites met Yahweh in both history and sacred story also produced symbols and rituals—their forms of sacraments. The symbolic actions and objects expressed the world view of a people who see themselves in a covenant with their god. All the Israelites' rituals, from their daily blessings to their most solemn occasions, attested to the significance of being in a covenant with Yahweh. All their practices call to

Mary G. Durkin

mind Yahweh's activity on their behalf. Retelling the story of the nation was an important part of every ritual.

Biblical scholars note that the Old Testament people viewed time and place as sacred, but not as magical. Rituals, objects and persons that commemorated this sacredness also had a sacramental quality. The Holy of Holies, the interior chamber of the temple, was sacred. So, too, were the temple priests who performed sacrificial rituals that put people in touch with Yahweh. The synagogue, where the focus was on interpreting and teaching the word of Yahweh, also had symbolic value.

The Passover was the prime example of the commemoration of sacred time. The retelling of the story reminded the Israelite of a Yahweh-God who acted in his people's past, acts in their present, and will continue to act in their future. The participants remembered why time was sacred and then remembered the role they were to play in the time-honored covenant. The Law contained the rules they were to follow to fulfill their part of the covenant. With special foods, blessings, and the retelling of the story, the ritual meal in the home captured the sacred history even as it acknowledged the important ritual of eating together.

Every so often, throughout its long history, the Israelite nation emphasized the details of the Law and the rituals, and paid little attention to the meaning behind them. The prophets often chastised the people for misuse of temple rituals and rites of purification, and for adhering to the letter of the law while ignoring the spirit. They were condemned for the *sacralized* practices that the people of Yahweh's covenant should oppose. These abuses were es-

The Eucharist

pecially prominent at the time of Jesus. He condemned those who put the Law before love. He also condemned those rituals that had magical connotations.

In summary, Jesus and his early followers came from a religious tradition that, while not using the word sacrament, made use of symbolic actions and objects to give meaning to human experience. This tradition, with its emphasis on God speaking through people and events, found sacred meaning in the actions of these events and in the books that recorded these actions. Of particular importance to the Christian notion of sacrament is the role remembrance played in the Israelite religion. The domestic rituals that point to the sacredness of all experience, the emphasis in the synagogue on the word of God, and the importance of the temple priest and of sacrifice, all contributed as well to the Christian development of sacraments.

New Testament Beginnings

Before reviewing New Testament writings about sacramental activities, it is important to note that these writings describe the experiences of Jesus' earliest followers. Though there is some theological reflection in the retelling of these stories, it is very basic. The New Testament communities developed an initial theology by interpreting their experiences in the light of Jesus' teaching—or, more specifically, what they remembered of his teaching. The only theological framework available to those doing the inter-

Mary G. Durkin

preting was their own perception of how the message of Jesus applied to their experiences. If a religious community does not have this close relationship between faith and experience, then their sacraments fail to answer the meaningful questions of the community.

The word *sacrament* does not appear in the New Testament. There are records of rituals that would qualify as sacraments, but there is neither a general nor a generic sense of the word in reference to these rituals. Confusion among later scholars about the presence of the word in the New Testament resulted from misunderstandings in translations.

Paul used the word *mysterion* in his writings when referring to something hidden or secret. For example, he sees God's plan of salvation as *mysterion*. He also sees wisdom as *mysterion*, revealed only to those who are spiritual. In addition, Paul's own message and the Spirit's role in making Christ known are labelled *mysterion*. No New Testament writer use this term when referring to the rituals associated with the seven sacraments that exist today.

The early Greek Christians, however, began to use the word *mysterion* to describe their rituals. They undoubtedly borrowed it from the mystery cults of the Greek culture. The translation problem began when subsequent Latin translations of the Bible sometimes translated *mysterion* as *sacramentum*. This translation led to confusion among later theologians. Relying on the Latin translations of the Bible, they found what they thought were specific uses of the word *sacrament* in the New Testament.

There were two meanings for the term *sacramentum* in

The Eucharist

the common usage of the time. First, it referred to the oath of loyalty taken by a soldier and to oaths in general which consecrated the oath and the oath-taker to the gods. The second use of the term referred to the money deposited in the temple by both parties in a civil suit and surrendered to the state by the losing party. When the Latin Fathers found the word, they associated it with these meanings.

Though not using the term *sacramentum,* the New Testament does contain accounts of various rituals that symbolized God's presence in the community. The early Christians ate meals in common. At these meals, they shared bread and wine in memory of Jesus and felt at one with him. They often engaged in a ritual washing after listening to the disciples preach the word of God. Following the experience of the Spirit at Pentecost, they practiced a laying on of hands in which others were filled with a new spirit and spoke in tongues.

In *Clothed in Christ,* Downey maintains that the New Testament rituals represent a historical and eschatological (toward final fulfillment) view of faith, salvation, and worship. The cross and resurrection were the sign of God's activity in the person of Jesus. Belief in both the cross and resurrection brought the early Christians together for worship. The rituals of this period centered around proclamation of the word, telling of what God had done in Jesus, and prayers of thanksgiving and blessing.

The Christians replaced the highly developed ritual practices of the Jewish religion with what Downey calls a *desacralized* worship. The community moved from temple sacrifice to meal of memory and thanksgiving. The notion of

Mary G. Durkin

temple priest and priesthood gave way to the concept of a priestly people. Instead of offering a sacrifice, the community remembered Jesus' life and death and resurrection. Once again God's action in history, this time in the person of Jesus, became the sacrament.

The experiences of Jesus, remembered by his followers, gave meaning to their experiences. Because he was the one God made present to them, he was an opaque sign, able to be understood by a community that interpreted his meaning. Jesus lived on in the community of believers. The New Testament accounts of Jesus and of the early Church contain the seeds of the subsequent development of a sacramental system.

The Tradition

The story of that development covers a long period of Church history. The Church moved from a community with no clearly defined sacramental system to one with seven sacraments thought to be outward signs instituted by Christ. The Catholic notion of sacrament emerged over time as people interpreted the New Testament in the light of cultural influences and challenges.

Layer upon layer of interpretation eventually led to a system that at times seemed far removed from its original roots. The development becomes clearer, however, if one views the various interpretations as responses to the experiences of the times. When discussing the sacraments, and specifically the Eucharist, contemporary Catholics benefit

The Eucharist

from knowing how the theology of sacraments developed in their Church and how the present system of sacraments came into existence.

The Patristic Period

Both the theological writings and the practices of the Patristic era reflect how the idea of sacrament developed as a response to and an adaptation of the culture.

The early Fathers of the Church, Justin, Irenaeus, and Clement of Alexandria, engaged in the most prominent second-century apologetics for Christianity. They defended their religion against the Greek mystery cults and Jewish and Gnostic teachings. In their writings, the word *mysterion* was used in several different ways. It was used to describe secret mystery cults. It was also used when referring to biblical events in which they saw the divine plan realized. In addition, they applied it to events in Jesus' life.

In the Latin Church of the third century, Tertullian applied the word *sacramentum* to Baptism and the Eucharist. The concept of the soldier's oath influenced his view of Baptism as the means by which the Christian, who pledges allegiance to Christ, is consecrated to God. At that time, the baptized person was an adult who could make this pledge. For Tertullian, the Eucharist was a *signifying* ritual whereby God *sanctified* Christians through the person of Jesus. Cyprian of Carthage continued this view of the Eucharist as both signifying and sanctifying. It was developed still further by St. Augustine.

Mary G. Durkin

Augustine's reflections led to a turning point in sacramental thinking. His major contribution was to introduce the idea of sacrament as sacred sign. Within his neo-Platonic theory of symbols, *sacramentum* is a species of the family of symbols. A sacrament belongs to divine things and has to do with the realm of the sacred.

According to Augustine, a sign is a thing that, apart from its appearance to the senses, causes something more to come to mind. There are natural signs and there are things that become signs by the free choice of the individual. Like the symbols mentioned earlier, these free choice signs are symbols referring to that which they signify. In addition, the signified can itself become a symbol.

He categorized the relationship between a sign and what it signifies in three ways. First, there is what is seen and what is. There is also what is seen and what is understood. Finally, there is what is seen and what is believed.

For Augustine, the two sacraments of Baptism and Eucharist were sacred signs of grace. He saw an analogy to nature in these sacraments. The water of Baptism symbolized the inner cleansing that took place in the person being baptized. The grains of wheat in the bread symbolized the members of the body of Christ.

The sacraments, however, were more than analogies to nature, more than just interpretive symbols. The sacramental rituals also effected, or brought about, what they symbolized. In Baptism, the person experiences cleansing faith. The Eucharist gave the unifying power of body and blood of Christ. For the Christian the most important

The Eucharist

thing was that what is signified is effected by Christ.

In summing up the sacramental practices of this Patristic period, Downey uses the words *adaptation* and *resacralization*. During this time, there was a return of cult and priest as well as a sense of awe and fear of sacred things and people. The Christians who originally desacralized the pagan, magical abuses that crept into Judaism now experienced a similar attraction to cult and priest. This resacralization, as explained below, was closely linked to the adaptation occurring at the same time. Both of these phenomena affected the later development of the sacramental system.

One example of the adaptation occurring during this period was the move from the domestic setting to the basilica for worship. As membership in the Christian community increased, the community outgrew the house-church as a place of worship. Christians began using larger, public buildings for community worship. Initially, the building itself did not have a sacred significance, though it eventually acquired one.

When the state granted recognition to the Christian faith, Roman influences led to sacralization of rituals. Worship came to be seen as sacrifice. Because of this emphasis on sacrifice, the bishop, with his priestly character, began to be distinguished from the body of the faithful. The basilica became a sacred place because the sacred activity of the bishop-priest offering a sacrifice took place there.

Another example of adaptation can be found in the vari-

Mary G. Durkin

ety of eucharistic prayers which appeared in this period. The prayers of different Christian communities emerged from their different needs and understandings of Christ and his mysteries. The prayers used the experiences of each community to express the meaning of Christ for its members.

The complexity of the sacramental question during this period is evident in the symbolic sensibility of many writers. Some of the Fathers saw a real participation in the mystery of Christ in the sacramental ritual. When they wrote about sacraments, they were referring to more than seven sacraments and more than ritual actions. They spoke of feasts of the Church year, reading and proclaiming the gospel, prayers of blessing, Christ, the Church, ritual acts, lives of Christian people, the Scriptures and icons. All of these were reminders of the mystery of Christ.

Other writers, however, showed a loss of symbolic sensibility. Resacralization sometimes led to the symbol becoming a veil covering the higher realities it represented. Thus, the liturgy became overdramatized with an emphasis on objects, actions, gestures, or words rather than on their meaning for the community. Overawe of the sacred put a barrier between the people and the message of the faith.

At the conclusion of this period, the Church still had not developed the system of seven sacraments, nor a theology to support such a system. Indeed, there was no widely accepted, precise definition of sacrament. The Church existed for twelve centuries before such a definition was proposed and accepted.

The Eucharist
The Middle Ages

From the sixth to the twelfth centuries, sacramental practices developed considerably. Both the ritual forms and the meanings of the symbols evolved over time. Baptism and Confirmation became separate rites. The Eucharist shifted in emphasis from fellowship meal to a highly clerical ritual with scant lay participation. Private confession rather than public penance became the norm. The ordination process began to include a series of holy orders. Marriage came to be considered a sacrament; and anointing of the dying replaced anointing of the sick as a sacred ritual.

This drift away from patristic influences was not as obvious in the Eastern churches. By the twelfth century, however, the Western rites had become more or less standardized, with a liturgical style under the influence of Rome. The seven rites listed above were looked upon as the principal sacraments, although other practices were still called sacraments. Then, in the thirteenth century, the Church established a more limited definition of a sacrament. During the Second Council of Lyon (1274), the Church leadership specified which church rituals could be called sacraments.

Although sacramental practices continued to develop during the early Middle Ages, there was little corresponding development in sacramental theology from the time of Augustine to the beginning of the twelfth century. During that period, the Church struggled with the collapse of the Roman empire and Germanic invasions. It focused

Mary G. Durkin

much of its attention on missionary efforts to Christianize Europe.

Nevertheless, in the seventh century, Isidore of Seville claimed that a sacrament was a secret and sacred power hidden under visible actions. His perception led to the idea of a sacrament as a vessel of grace. For the next four centuries, Isidore of Seville's definition, rather than Augustine's, dominated the limited theological discussion of sacraments.

Then, in the eleventh century, Berengar of Tours proposed that a sacrament was a sacred sign. He used Augustine's theory of sacrament to support his own ideas on the Eucharist. Berengar, however, believed that the sign was not the thing signified. Nor was the symbol the thing symbolized. For Berengar, the sacrament was not the reality at all, but only a symbol. Rome rejected this notion of symbolism, espousing instead the realism of St. Augustine. In fact, the Church condemned as heretical Berengar's position that the bread and wine, after consecration, "is only sacrament and not the true body and blood of Our Lord Jesus Christ."

During the twelfth and thirteenth centuries, a period of relative peace and prosperity settled over Europe. Theological reflection began to flourish again. The stage was set once more for theology to evolve out of the sacramental practices of the time.

Early in the twelfth century, Hugo of St. Victor, a theologian at the University of Paris, defined sacraments as "receptacles of grace." He claimed that a sacrament was a sign of a sacred thing by which a visible reality seen exter-

The Eucharist

nally signified another invisible, interior reality. Sacraments remained different from signs, however. According to St. Victor, a sign could signify something but could not confer grace. A sacrament, on the other hand, could both signify something and efficaciously confer grace. St. Victor's concept of efficacy eventually became normative in the Church.

St. Victor's discussion of sacraments encompassed more than the seven rituals listed at the beginning of this chapter. He applied his notion of sacrament to, among other things, rituals and beliefs, the use of holy water and blessed ashes; the incarnation of Christ and the sign of the cross; and the vows, consecration, and burial of monks. St. Victor believed that the goal of all sacramental rites was to encourage the faithful by providing opportunities for the reception of grace. In addition, these rites could support the faithful in their moral growth.

Later in the century, Peter Lombard included a systematic treatment of the sacraments in what became his standard, widely-used textbook for theology students. He treated the seven principal Church rituals of his day. In his textbook, he defined a sacrament as a *sign* of the grace of God and a *form* of invisible grace which is both the image and the cause of that grace. This definition incorporated the earlier idea of efficacious grace. It subsequently became the normative understanding of sacrament within the Church. The seven sacraments were considered causes as well as signs of grace. Once again, however, all signs were not sacraments. Because sacramentals did not cause grace, they were only signs.

Mary G. Durkin

Twelfth-century scholastic theology, based on the works of Aristotle, accepted this fairly standard understanding of sacraments. While scholars at that time disagreed over peripheral matters, they agreed that sacraments were both the sign and the cause of grace.

How the sacraments caused grace became the subject of debate, however. The theories proposed fell into three categories: (1) instrumental, efficient causality; (2) moral causality; and (3) occasional causality. No one theory has ever received official Church sanction. Prior to the Second Vatican Council, the first position, usually known as the theory of instrumental, efficient causality, held sway. It was advocated by St. Thomas Aquinas.

Aquinas argued that a sacred sign is only a sacrament if it sanctifies, that is gives grace. A sign sanctifies as God's instrument, not simply by its external rite. According to Aquinas, there are three causes of sanctification: the passion of Christ, grace, and external life. God, however, is the ultimate cause of sanctification.

But if God saves, why do people still needs signs? Aquinas offered three reasons: (1) by their nature, humans need to be led by bodily and sensible reality to nonsensible, intelligible, spiritual reality; (2) through sin, humans become subjected to sensible reality, making the remedies of sin come through that same sensible reality; and (3) human activity makes it difficult to abstract from bodily reality, so spiritual reality can only intrude through bodily realities.

Most Thomistic theologians interpret him as saying that God is the primary effecting agent of the sacrament. The

The Eucharist

rite, the prescribed form of the sacrament, is only an instrumental and secondary agent, working under the influence of God. Still, in the effect, something can be attributed to the instrument as cause. Thus a sacrament is both a cause and a sign. As a cause, it effects grace. As a sign, it produces knowledge of its effect. Therefore, what is said about sacraments as effect is quite different from what is said about sacraments as cause. This distinction between the sign and the cause of sacraments has continued in the Catholic Church until the recent past.

St. Thomas also considered how the sacraments could be imbued with divine power. He maintained that Christ becomes present through a sacrament because the priest performing the rite has been invested with power and authority through ordination. Moreover, he believed that the Word of God, which has its own power, supports the basic form of the sacramental rituals. For example, the water in Baptism and the bread and wine in the Eucharist have power because these objects are used in the rituals that are found in the New Testament.

Alexander of Hales, writing before St. Thomas, laid the groundwork for the second explanation as to how sacraments cause grace. Alexander observed that sacraments cause an effect in the soul. This observation led to the theory of occasional causality, which states that God determines the occasion on which he alone confers grace. St. Bonaventure, a Scholastic theologian of St. Thomas' era, advanced the theory of occasional causality when he claimed that sacraments cause grace by divine institution. For Bonaventure, divine power always effects grace in any-

Mary G. Durkin

one who receives a sacrament worthily. John Duns Scotus, writing in the thirteenth century, argued further that sacraments are necessary to free people from sin. The sacraments gain significance through the authority God gives to the occasion, conferring grace in an efficient way.

The third view of sacramental causality—moral causality—also grew out of Scholastic thought. The theory of moral causality interpreted sacraments as a pleading with God for grace. The causal action of the sacrament is on God, who then produces the effect. From this perspective, a sacramental rite is seen as a pleading prayer, oriented to God rather than to the recipient.

The practices of the thirteenth century Church reflected the theological definition of sacrament and the theoretical separation of cause and effect in sacraments. The theories de-emphasized the previous symbolic sensitivity towards the sacraments.

At that time, the model for ordering society was hierarchical: heaven above, earth in the middle, and hell below. Everything in between was assigned its proper place according to a prior ordination by God. As such, the Church was considered the perfect society, a model of hierarchy at work.

Within this perfect society, the priest was the focus of sacramental life. By the power of his ordination, he mediated between the sacred and the temporal orders. Nonordained Catholics became passive observers in this arrangement, receiving the sacraments rather than participating in them. The sacraments stopped being communal activities and became things. People were told that

The Eucharist

the sacraments were visible signs of invisible grace. Sacramental rituals therefore became mere instruments, reminders of devotion to something beyond them.

Since the authorities guaranteed Christ's presence in the sacraments, there was little need for Catholics to understand the nature and quality of the symbols and rituals. Christ's presence in a sacrament depended solely on the correct exercise of the priest's power. For this reason, sacramental rituals began to be seen as magical routines evoking automatic responses. This emphasis on magic spread to other devotions. Novenas, pilgrimages, relics, aspirations, and donations for prayers for the dead were among the many unofficial and unsanctioned practices of the day which were thought to bring special favors from God.

The understanding of sacraments which developed in the Middle Ages and the implications of that understanding influenced the Church's sacramental system until the time of Vatican II. Contemporary Catholics still experience the consequences of this ordered, medieval world view, particularly those Catholics who grew up before the liturgical reforms. If the symbols in the sacrament do not matter, then the liturgical actions are unimportant. If the priest alone mediates the presence of Christ in the exercise of his ordained ministry, then he alone becomes the focal point of the liturgy. The laity turns to devotional practices to experience more directly God's presence.

In sum, the theology and practices of the Middle Ages, without the corrections of earlier periods in Church history, led to a sacramental system that was insensitive to

Mary G. Durkin

both the power of symbols and people's need for symbols. This insensitivity eventually demanded corrective action.

The Reformation/Trent

Between the twelfth century and the early sixteenth century, nine general councils dealt with the clerical and political abuses that had developed in the Church. Among the more flagrant abuses that they never successfully eradicated were practices that directly or indirectly affected the sacramental life of the Church. Priests, ordained by bishops appointed by kings, often administered sacraments for a fee. After canon law mandated celibacy, some bishops sold their priests licenses to have concubines. Bishops appointed relatives, sometimes their own sons, to succeed them. Popes and bishops lived in luxury, with the popes taxing the bishops and the bishops taxing the people. The people lived in poverty and ignorance, which in turn encouraged fear and superstition.

At the same time, a new sense of nationalism and humanism emerged as well as a new birth of culture. The Europe that developed from this combination challenged the authority of the abuse-filled Catholic Church.

The resulting Reformation and Counter-Reformation sparked a re-evaluation of the sacraments. Protestants rejected the Catholic system, which they saw as non-biblical and filled with superstition. In response, the Catholic Church defended its system of seven sacraments in the medieval tradition.

The Reformers wanted individuals to have a direct rela-

The Eucharist

tionship with God—without any church intervening and hindering immediate access to God. They also wanted theology to make experiential as well as logical sense.

They found the scholastic synthesis of the sacramental system inadequate for their experiences. They observed little if any spiritual effect on those who participated in sacraments that the Church claimed had a spiritual effect. They questioned the lack of biblical evidence for some sacramental rites practiced by the Catholic Church. They did find biblical evidence, however, to support the belief that at least two visible ceremonies were instituted by Christ—Baptism and Eucharist. In the countries where the Reform movement took root, most Catholic sacramental practices were abolished or at least simplified.

Reformers interpreted the meaning of the two remaining rituals in different ways. Theologies varied according to the different experiences on which they were based. Some reformation theologies adopted symbolism in their approach to the sacraments while others found the concept of realism more effective. Most of the reform positions fell into one of three categories, however, as illustrated by the teachings of three major reformers: Luther, Calvin, and Zwingli.

Luther's position represents the views of those who held that sacraments had divine effects. He agreed with Augustine's realism and maintained that sacraments had an effective character. And yet, according to Luther, it is God alone who works in the proclamation of the Word and in the sacraments. The human participant in the sacrament remains necessarily open and receptive but can do nothing

Mary G. Durkin

unless God causes faith and pledges salvation.

Luther believed that faith had priority over everything else. Sacraments were valid only in the context of faith. The only authority was the Word of God in Scripture—not the power of the priest or the authority of the Church. Luther placed Scripture in the hands of the people and established a form of group worship which focused on proclamation, narrative, and commemoration. Central to this worship was his belief in the priesthood of all who assemble and who remember the one hoped for in the breaking of the bread and the sharing of the cup.

In contrast, Calvin supported the position that sacraments have human effects. He contended that God alone is the subject of sacraments. Through the sacraments of Baptism and Eucharist, God seals his promises and strengthens the faith of believers. Calvin did not agree with Luther on the subordination of sacraments to the Word. In addition, Calvin emphasized the role of the Holy Spirit as mediator in the sacraments. The Holy Spirit makes possible the link between the heavenly Christ and the earthly bread and wine received by the individual. Without faith, which is the gift of the Spirit, the sacraments would be empty symbols.

Zwingli believed that the sacraments had no effects. He considered the word *sacrament* unbiblical and rejected it. His sacramental symbolism embraced the ritual acts of Baptism and the Lord's Supper (the Reformers' designation of the Eucharist) as symbols—and symbols only—of a spiritual reception of salvation. When these rituals commemorate the redeeming acts of Christ, they serve as signs of faith.

The Eucharist

The Council of Trent responded to the sacramental challenges of the Reformation by condemning specific errors of the Reformers and by attempting to eliminate the Church's own abuses. It legislated practical reforms that eradicated most of the abuses associated with the sacraments, especially those related to Penance and the Mass. For the first time, the Church developed a comprehensive, dogmatic doctrine of sacraments. The seven sacraments were clearly defined as official Church rituals.

The positions advocated by the Council, however, furthered the legalistic and hierarchical tendencies of the Middle Ages. To reassert the validity of the Church's sacramental system, the Council appealed to divine and priestly authority and power. The following specific declarations of the Council indirectly imposed a standard sacramental practice and theology on all Catholicism:

- The sacraments are instituted by Christ.
- There are seven sacraments.
- Sacraments confer grace.
- Sacraments are symbols of sacred things.
- Three sacraments bestow an indelible character on the soul and can be received only once.
- Sacraments are necessary for salvation.
- Grace is always offered even though individuals might set up obstacles to receiving it.
- Grace is conferred by the rite itself, not by the faith of the recipient or worthiness of the minister.
- The minister must intend to follow what the Church declares to be the true rite for it to be effective.

Mary G. Durkin

Following the Council, there were reforms in canon law which imposed even greater uniformity on Catholic sacramental practices. The Roman missal and the Roman sacramentaries, which contain the words and rubric (directions) for all the sacraments, became standard. As a result, few Catholics saw the need for any alternative interpretation of the meaning or practice of the sacraments. The Council effectively settled the central issues of the sacramental system for the next four centuries.

Contemporary Discussions

During the first half of the twentieth century, Catholic parents felt confident that they were passing on the faith as it had always been and always would be. When they listened to their school-age children recite the definition of a sacrament from *The Baltimore Catechism,* they rarely, if ever, thought to question the biblical, historical, or symbolic validity of what they were hearing.

The Church developed a fortress mentality after the Council of Trent. Continually on the defensive, the Church allowed little opportunity for individual members to question how the sacraments related to human experience. The Church taught what was necessary for salvation, and the laity, for the most part, went along with these teachings. Most Catholics, including Church leaders, came to believe that the sacramental system—as they knew it—had been ordained by Christ during his ministry here on earth.

The Eucharist

The Council of Trent curtailed almost any creative thinking about the sacraments. By the late nineteenth century, however, a number of ideas came together which influenced Catholic thinkers. They were encouraged to begin re-examining the Church's sacramental theology and practices. Most Catholics were unaware that movements both in the Church and in the culture at large would soon have a considerable effect on the Catholic understanding of sacraments.

Neoscholasticism and liturgical and scriptural renewal created interest in the biblical, patristic, and medieval treatment of sacraments. Scholars who had access to original works of scripture and who were cognizant of the cultural influences on these works began asking questions about the meaning of traditional sacramental teachings. They observed that legalistic and mechanistic attitudes had made the sacraments unresponsive to human experience. They wanted to study the origins of the sacraments, to uncover the human experiences that had first inspired these traditional theological formulations and practices.

The Church regularly appealed to Tradition to validate its teachings and its sacramental system. It therefore created the impression that it had always held these same positions. Scholars discovered, to the contrary, that both sacramental theology and sacramental practice had developed over time. The review in these early chapters of the place of symbol in human experience and the evolution of the sacramental tradition illustrates this development. The experience of sacraments in the past turned out to be dif-

Mary G. Durkin

ferent from what people had thought it to be. This discovery led to theological and liturgical renewal.

These scholarly movements and a variety of cultural and social forces at work in the twentieth-century world were behind Vatican II's attempt in the 1960s to make the Church responsive to the modern world. The Council, in turn, became the vehicle for making known the new understanding of sacraments which had been developing in the previous fifty years.

The Council described the Church as the People of God and thus opened sacramental life and worship to general participation. Liturgical reforms such as the use of the vernacular, a new responsiveness to local customs, and the establishment of non-ordained ministries caused both laity and clergy to take a new look at the role of sacraments. When change became possible in that which was once thought unchangeable, many other questions surfaced.

For instance, the Council's attempt at ecumenical dialogue, though limited, highlighted the need for a better understanding of the differences in sacramental perspectives. Since the Council ended, the sacramental, theological, and liturgical renewal that helped shape the Council's vision has evolved even further.

Current theological literature includes a variety of descriptions of the sacraments. In addition to being seen as symbolic actions, the sacraments have also been defined as encounters with God, celebrations of life, signs of grace, and the communal participation in Jesus' worship of the Father. Behind almost all theological and liturgical discus-

The Eucharist

sions of the sacraments is a common desire to correlate experience and faith. While many of the theoretical and practical discussions have not produced sacramental practices that make this correlation obvious, the aim is still a worthy one.

Two of these contemporary theoretical discussions are of particular importance: (1) the idea of Jesus as the primordial Sacrament and (2) the examination of the Catholic religious heritage and imagination.

Edward Schillebeeckx, Karl Rahner, and Bernard Cooke are among the theologians responsible for the view that Jesus is the primordial Sacrament. This notion is central to contemporary sacramental theology and practice. It can be summarized as follows: Jesus is the sacrament of God, the Church is the sacrament of Jesus, and individual Christians are sacraments for the Church to the rest of the world.

Schillebeeckx, interpreting Thomas Aquinas through the perspective of existentialism, sees Jesus as the sacrament through which his followers encountered the mystery of God. Even after his death and resurrection, Jesus remained the one who revealed the transcendent God to those who accepted his message. The community of those who believe in him then became a sacrament for others. The seven sacraments are encounters with Christ made available through Church rituals that have changed over the centuries since that initial encounter with Jesus.

Karl Rahner, using a phenomenological analysis, developed a theory of sacraments as symbols of the grace of

Mary G. Durkin

self-transcendence made possible by Christ. Sacraments are possible because Christ instituted a sacramental Church. Therefore, sacraments express the nature of the Church and are also signs and means of grace for those who participate fully in them.

Rahner did not deny the traditional teachings on sacraments but, by using a different analysis, attempted to end the separation of sacraments as signs and as causes. Thus, sacraments can be symbolic activities for communities and for individuals, helping them realize who they are and what they are to be as people saved by God's grace—of which Christ is the perfect human incarnation.

For Bernard Cooke, the purpose of sacraments is the transformation of fundamental human experiences. Jesus made this transformation possible because he gave all human experience new meaning by the way he lived in God's intimate presence. His whole life, but especially his death and resurrection, was sacramental.

According to Cooke, Jesus instituted the sacraments not by directly choosing specific rituals but by being—in life, death, and resurrection—the primordial sacrament of his Father's saving presence. The believing community of the Church preserves the significance of Jesus' passage through death to new life. Thus, the Church is the sacrament of Christ who himself is the sacrament of his Father.

Theologian Lawrence Cunningham and sociologist of religion Andrew Greeley indirectly contribute to the contemporary discussion of sacraments through their analysis of the Catholic religious heritage and the Catholic religious imagination. Their work shows how pervasive the sacra-

The Eucharist

mental mentality is to those who have grown up exposed to the Catholic experience. The idea that God is present not only in the seven key moments of the sacraments but also in a variety of human experiences is basic to a Catholic understanding of the meaning of life. The Sacraments (with a capital S) of the Church have nurtured this sacramental view of life—a natural outcome of the Catholic positions on Creation, Incarnation, Redemption, Spirit, and Grace.

Ecumenical dialogue on the sacraments and the contemporary liturgical movement have also had an impact on how contemporary Catholics view the sacraments. Most ecumenical discussions on sacraments focus on Baptism and the Eucharist, although some explore ministry as well. To find areas of agreement, the churches involved in these discussions must continually re-examine and refine their own attitudes on these sacraments. The emphasis on Church as sacrament also broadens the areas for dialogue.

The contemporary liturgical movement strives to develop alternative experiences of worship which will speak to the variety of human experiences. Participants in these liturgies, however, often discover that rituals developed in a vacuum become mere signs. Though the majority of contemporary Catholics are satisfied with the new liturgy, most Church rituals fall far short of encouraging an ongoing correlation of life and faith.

Nevertheless, armed with contemporary scientific insights about human experience and the fruits of biblical and historical research, students of both sacramental theology and liturgy can take advantage of opportunities to

Mary G. Durkin

deepen the People of God's appreciation of the sacraments.

Summary

This review of the origins and history of the Catholic sacraments shows how varying interpretations and their practical consequences contributed to the sacramental system in its past and present states. The evolution from simple biblical practices to the elaborate system of the late Middle Ages demonstrates how understanding and practice respond to cultural influences. The Council of Trent was itself a response to Reformers' critiques of sacramental abuses. Unfortunately, it led to stagnation in sacramental liturgy and theology for more than three centuries and attests to the ongoing need for correlating life and faith.

Contemporary Catholics studying the Eucharist would do well to bear in mind this historical development of sacraments in the Church. They would then be able to examine the distinctive features of this core sacrament against the backdrop of all the sacraments and within the sacramental framework of Catholicism.

PART TWO

THE HISTORY

CHAPTER THREE

The Eucharist: Its Beginnings

Now as they were eating, Jesus took bread, and when he had said the blessing he broke it and gave it to the disciples. "Take it and eat," he said, "this is my body." Then he took a cup, and when he had given thanks he handed it to them saying, "Drink from this, all of you, for this is my blood, the blood of the covenant, poured out for many for the forgiveness of sins. From now on, I tell you, I shall never again drink wine until the day I drink the new wine with you in the kingdom of my Father.

Matthew 26:26-29

And as they were eating he took bread, and when he had said the blessing he broke it and gave it to them. "Take it," he said, "this is my body." Then he took a cup, and

Mary G. Durkin

when he had given thanks he handed it to them, and all drank from it, and he said to them, "This is my blood, the blood of the covenant, poured out for many. In truth I tell you, I shall never drink wine any more until the day I drink the new wine in the kingdom of God.

Mark 14:22-25

And he said to them, "I have ardently longed to eat this Passover with you before I suffer, because, I tell you, I shall not eat it until it is fulfilled in the kingdom of God." Then, taking a cup, he gave thanks and said, "Take this and share it among you, because from now on, I tell you, I shall never again drink wine until the kingdom of God comes." Then he took bread, and when he had given thanks, he broke it and gave it to them, saying, "This is my body given for you; do this in remembrance of me." He did the same with the cup after supper, and said, "This cup is the new covenant in my blood poured out for you.

Luke 22:15-20

For the tradition I received from the Lord and also handed on to you is that on the night he was betrayed, the Lord Jesus took some bread, and after he had given thanks, he broke it, and he said, "This is my body, which is for you; do this in remembrance of me." And in the same way, with the cup after supper, saying, "This cup is the new covenant in my blood. Whenever you drink it, do this as a memorial of me." Whenever you eat this bread,

The Eucharist

then, and drink this cup, you are proclaiming the Lord's death until he comes.

I Corinthians 11:23-26

MOST contemporary Catholics would be hard pressed to answer in a clear fashion the question "What is the Eucharist?" Those educated before Vatican II probably would fumble around before offering one of several views: "It's the sacrament in which the priest, through the power given him by Christ, changes bread and wine into the body and blood of Christ" or "It's what happens at the consecration" or "It's Communion or *Holy* Communion" or "It's the Blessed Sacrament" or "It's the continuation of Christ's sacrifice on the Cross" or, perhaps, "It's what takes place during the Sacrifice of the Mass." Younger Catholics might use some of the newer terminology—Eucharistic celebration, the liturgy, the gathering of the People of God. Some Catholics might simply reply, "Eucharist is the Mass." Others would not equate the Mass with the Eucharist.

If asked to explain the origins of the Eucharist, however, Catholics would respond with more unanimity. The standard response would be, "Christ instituted the Eucharist at the Last Supper." After all, the Canon of the Mass recalls that event for them. As additional proof that the Eucharist began with the Last Supper, Catholics might cite the Passion account they hear each year during Holy Week. That account testifies to the validity of what they re-create at the Mass. Some might even point to St. Paul's letter to the Co-

Mary G. Durkin

rinthians as evidence that the early followers of Jesus continued to do as he directed them to do at the Last Supper.

Theologians and liturgists who want to explain the meaning of the Eucharist also offer a variety of responses to the question "What is the Eucharist?" It is both an object and an action that is also a thanksgiving, a remembering, a sharing, a blessing, a sending forth, a dying, a living, and a call to commitment. To arrive at these various interpretations, the scholars appeal to the Bible and to Tradition, but not in the strictly literal sense of former times. Armed with the insights of biblical and historical research, they look at past events searching for what really happened. They also want to know the meaning of what happened.

Contemporary readers of the New Testament who are familiar with biblical research now know that the Gospels are not, nor were they intended to be, historically accurate accounts of the life of Jesus. Rather, they were a new literary device that wove together stories from the life of Jesus to meet the concerns of the Christian community. The Gospel writers were redactors rather than historians; they each wrote for the needs of their particular communities.

The first Gospel, Mark, appeared over thirty years after the death of Jesus. The last Gospel, John, probably dates from the end of the first century. Before the Gospels appeared, the early Christians developed an oral and liturgical tradition, revolving around the life of Jesus. The liturgical tradition incorporated the stories and sayings of the oral tradition. These traditions were the basis for the emerging New Testament accounts of the institution of the Eucharist.

The Eucharist

Today's readers of the New Testament also know that many of St. Paul's letters preceded the Gospel accounts. Nevertheless, the first of these letters did not appear until over fifteen years after the death of Jesus. By then, an oral tradition existed. His letters presumed the existence of this tradition. Paul did not always explain what his readers already knew.

For these reasons, any claims about the biblical foundations of the Eucharist must take into consideration the backgrounds of the various biblical communities. It is not enough to claim that the biblical account of the Last Supper supplies all one needs to know about the institution of the Eucharist. There are several accounts and there are differences in these accounts.

Xavier Léon-Dufour, a New Testament scholar, advises those who set out to investigate the biblical origins of the Eucharist that they should expect surprises. There are only a few direct references to this early Christian ritual in the New Testament, and when the word *eucharistia* appears, it does not refer to that ritual. The words used by the New Testament writers are "the Lord's Supper" and "the breaking of the bread." Also, the New Testament accounts of the Lord's Supper on the night he was betrayed are much less definitive when seen as part of the whole framework of the Gospel.

Thus, a reader of the New Testament should not expect to know all there is to know about the Eucharist from a simple reading of one of the four Gospel accounts of the Last Supper. Only Matthew, Mark, and Luke include the words associated with the institution of the Eucharist.

Mary G. Durkin

Moreover, the few references in Acts and those in the Pauline literature do not present a clear-cut picture of how the community interpreted what was going on. The community context of these biblical remarks, however, sheds light on what they may have meant.

Tad Guzie in *Jesus and the Eucharist* studies the Eucharist as symbol. He suggests that there are two critical questions to be asked by anyone trying to understand the many layers of this rich religious symbol. The first question is, What did Jesus and his disciples do? The second question is, What is the meaning of what they did?

Answers to both questions depend upon understanding the significance of Jesus' actions and those of his disciples, particularly in the light of their Jewish roots. Old Testament traditions, as well as the activities of Jewish groups at the time of Jesus, supply some of this background information. In those instances where the audience was Gentile, the Gospels were composed with a particular emphasis on the experiences of that community.

A good way to begin a study of the biblical roots of the Eucharist is with a review of the four "institution accounts" (Mark 14:22-25, Matthew 26:26-29, Luke 22:15-20, and I Corinthians 11:23-26) and of the different presentation of the Last Supper in John's Gospel (which has no institution narrative). Certain themes emerge from this analysis which explain why contemporary liturgists and theologians interpret the Eucharist as they do. In addition, reviewing other New Testament accounts of Jesus' life from a eucharistic perspective sheds light both on what

The Eucharist

Jesus and his disciples were doing and on what it meant to them.

What Did Jesus Do?

The four Gospel writers and Paul all agree on one fact: Jesus shared a meal with his disciples on the night he was betrayed. Whether that meal was a Passover meal (the Synoptic Gospels) or a ritual meal prior to the Passover (John's account) is a subject of debate among biblical scholars. In either case, the context of the Supper and of the events following it has strong links with the Passover. Jesus gave a new interpretation, however, to what took place during the traditional meal.

Biblical scholars note that the institution accounts are substantially the same in all four renditions. They believe these accounts come from already existing liturgical practices. The Christian communities were already celebrating a remembrance of the Lord's Supper by the time these accounts appeared. The similarities in Matthew and Mark suggest that they were familiar with the same liturgical tradition, most likely the practices of Palestinian Christians in Jerusalem. Luke and Paul, in his First Letter to the Corinthians, most likely based their accounts on the Hellenistic observances of the Church in Antioch.

In all four accounts, Jesus takes bread, gives thanks (blesses it), breaks it, and gives it to his disciples (Paul does not mention the distribution, but it is implied). In Luke and Paul, Jesus admonishes his apostles to "do this as a memorial of me (in remembrance of me)."

Mary G. Durkin

In Mark and Matthew's accounts, Jesus then takes the cup of wine, blesses it, distributes it, and says, "This is my blood, the blood of the covenant, poured out for many." Matthew added the phrase "for the forgiveness of sins." In Luke and in Paul, this blessing of the cup takes place "after supper."

For Luke, this is the second thanksgiving Jesus says over a cup. Luke begins his institution account with Jesus declaring that he will not eat a Passover again "until it is fulfilled in the kingdom of God." Jesus than takes a cup, gives thanks, and states that he "shall never again drink wine until the kingdom of God comes." This assertion is followed by the words of institution over the bread. Then after the supper, Jesus again takes another cup, gives thanks, and explains that this cup is "the new covenant in my blood poured out for you." Matthew and Mark place Jesus' prediction about not drinking again until he is "in the kingdom of God" immediately after Jesus' words about the "blood of the covenant poured out for many."

The Gospel of John devotes five chapters (John 13-17) to the Last Supper yet makes no reference to the blessing of bread and wine or to Jesus' words over them. One theory regarding this omission holds that John's audience was already familiar with the liturgical practice recorded in the other Gospels.

John's Gospel develops a theory of the Eucharist in an earlier context, however. If John's audience was familiar with his theory as well as with the liturgical practice of the Lord's Supper, they would not have needed the theory re-

The Eucharist

peated in the Supper account. Thus, Chapter Six of John's Gospel—the story of the multiplication of the loaves and fishes—helps explain what at first seems a glaring omission in his description of the Last Supper.

The story of the multiplication of the loaves and fishes epitomizes the understanding of the Eucharist in the Gospel of John. In this account, Jesus' discourse on the bread of life (6:32-72) is an example of redaction at work. It illustrates how the Gospel writer may have revised or edited his material based upon his knowledge of his audience and their experiences. Verses 51-58, the most eucharistic passages of this discourse, undoubtedly reflect what Christians at the end of the first century believed about the bread and wine they used in their rituals. This eucharistic theology provides the basis for John's Last Supper account in Chapters 13-17.

It is impossible to state exactly what happened during the final meal Jesus shared with his closest followers. However, readers familiar with the practices of the Jewish communities at the time of Jesus would not be surprised by reports of the blessings (thanksgivings), the breaking of bread, or the sharing of the cup. They would be surprised at Jesus' emphasis on *my* body and *my* blood and the twist his words gave to the familiar ritual practices.

The breaking of bread in the Jewish community usually referred to the opening ceremony of a ritual meal. The head of the family took bread, said the blessing, broke the bread, and then shared it. In this Jewish meal, the breaking of the bread was accompanied by a thanksgiving prayer or

Mary G. Durkin

grace in which those present remembered, confessed, and proclaimed what Yahweh had done for his people.

The ritual meals of those who met in fellowship before the Sabbath and religious feasts also included prayers of blessing over each kind of food and a concluding prayer of thanksgiving, often over wine. Jesus and the Twelve would have followed these practices at their ritual meals.

The Passover was the most important ritual meal of the ancient Jewish community. It celebrated Yahweh's passing over of the Jewish first-born children when he slew the Egyptian first-born and led the Israelites out of slavery and through the Red Sea to freedom.

Chapter 12 of Exodus describes the ritual slaying of the lamb on Passover. It recounts the angel's instructions to put the blood on the doorpost, and it details how to prepare the unleavened bread and how to eat the lamb and bread.

Each spring, the ancient Jews re-enacted the events leading up to and following their freedom from slavery. The ritual celebration began with a blessing praising and thanking God and a blessing of a first cup. The opening ceremony also included a purification ritual and the eating of bitter herbs, a reminder of their ancestors' slavery.

The story of the first Passover was then read, followed by a meal of roasted lamb, unleavened bread, and cup of wine. Additional prayers of blessing and thanksgiving were offered over the food. The meal was followed by the blessing of a third cup. A psalm of praise concluded the celebration.

The Passover was a symbolic memorial ritual that made

The Eucharist

the past present to those who participated in the meal. They also experienced Yahweh's presence in a special way during this celebration. It reminded the participants of how they had been saved and of the meaning of that salvation. It strengthened their awareness of themselves as a people chosen by Yahweh.

Jesus and the Twelve, as well as the early Jewish Christians, would have been familiar with both the ritual and the meaning of the Passover celebration. They would have known the significance of the various blessings, thanksgivings, and praises used during the Passover celebration and at the fellowship meals they attended.

The New Testament accounts of the Last Supper answer the question "What did Jesus do?" by painting a picture of a familiar ritual meal with at least some reference to the Passover motif. As in most of the biblical stories, however, Jesus shatters the expectations of those around him. By referring to the bread and wine as *my* body and *my* blood, by equating these elements with the (new) covenant, by predicting his impending death, and by urging those with him to "do this in remembrance of me," Jesus set the stage for a dramatic eucharistic liturgy.

Scholars are not sure what portions of the biblical accounts detail what actually occurred at that last meal and what portion is the result of later reflection by Jesus' followers. Still, these reports of the Last Supper do recount the beginnings of the eucharistic liturgy. They also reveal what the earliest Christian community believed about Jesus' continuing presence in their midst.

Mary G. Durkin
What Did the Followers of Jesus Do?

The Gospels record that Jesus appeared to his followers after his death and resurrection. The Gospels describe several appearances at gatherings that may have been similar to the fellowship meals Jesus had once attended with his disciples. Once his appearances stopped, his followers continued to gather in weekly fellowship meals where they broke bread and shared the cup in memory of him. As they retold stories of the events associated with Jesus' Last Supper and his subsequent death and resurrection, they experienced his presence in much the same way as they had experienced Yahweh's presence in the Passover ritual.

Initially, these Christians also attended temple and synagogue services. The fellowship meals, however, were separate from these regular Jewish practices. The Epistles of St. Paul, especially the First Letter to the Corinthians, and the Acts of the Apostles contain the earliest direct references to Christian practices that are eucharistic in character.

In Corinth in the early years of the sixth decade of the first century, a community of Jesus' followers gathered regularly for a meal at which they celebrated the Lord's Supper, one of the two designations given to the ritual in the New Testament (Luke uses the term the breaking of the bread). In the culture of that era, communal meals were an established part of religious and social life. The Jewish community in Corinth gathered for religious communal meals. Other religious groups, as well as pagan and economic associations also met for communal meals. Gener-

The Eucharist

ally, these Jewish and pagan meals attracted members of a similar social or religious status (for example, Pharisees would gather with other Pharisees).

What distinguished the gatherings of Christians in Corinth, however, was that different social classes joined together for meals. Scholars surmise that the meals were eaten in the homes of the more well-to-do members of the community, who supplied the food for those less affluent.

Paul, hearing of the abuses that began to take place at these meals, wrote to the people of his concerns (I Corinthians 11). His letter indicates that some members were getting drunk on the wine. Others failed to share the food they brought for the feast with those less fortunate.

Paul reminded the Corinthian Christians that they were not to form separate little groups, refusing to share with one another. If their gatherings were simply for partying, then they were not participating in the Lord's Supper, a commemoration of Jesus' death as well as a celebration of his resurrection. Those who ate of the bread and drank of the cup were to be mindful of what they were doing. Only then would they realize that in the sharing of the bread and wine they were reminding one another of their unity in the body of Christ.

The Acts of the Apostles also contains a direct reference to early eucharistic practices. It cites a gathering that took place "in the houses" of the first Christians in Jerusalem (Acts 2:46). At this gathering, Christians took part in "The Breaking of Bread." Those who met together were the first converts who "remained faithful to the teaching of the apostles, to the brotherhood, to the breaking of the bread

Mary G. Durkin

and to the prayers" (Acts 2:42). They also shared everything in common and distributed among themselves, according to need, the proceeds of the sale of their possessions.

Later, in Acts 20, a gathering for the breaking of bread is described as taking place in Troas on what is now the northwest coast of Turkey. Paul preached a sermon at this gathering, which was held on the first day of the week. Scholars suggest that, by this time, Christians were holding their ritual meal on Sunday, the first day of the week, because it was the day of the Lord's resurrection. Following Jewish custom, however, they counted sundown of the previous day as the beginning of their Sabbath. Paul's preaching, most likely begun after sunset, continued until the middle of the night. It was interrupted when a young man (who had dozed off) fell three floors from his seat on a windowsill. Paul revived the dead man and returned to the gathering where "he broke bread and ate and carried on talking till he left at daybreak" (Acts 20:7-12).

These isolated New Testament references to early eucharistic practices illustrate how difficult it would be to use the New Testament as the sole guide to planning a liturgy. In none of these accounts is the word *eucharist* even applied to the entire rite. Scholars believe that in those instances when the term Eucharist is used, it keeps its Jewish meaning of "a thanksgiving filled with praise." The first mention of Eucharist associated with the entire ritual occurs in the *Didache,* a treatise which some biblical scholars believe predates the Gospel of John.

The Eucharist

Chapters Nine and Ten of the *Didache* contain a eucharistic formula that may or may not have been part of a eucharistic ritual. It might have applied only to a meal and did not include the actual words of institution. The formula outlines the thanks that is to be given with the cup and with the broken bread. Then, only those who are baptized are to eat or drink of the bread and cup. After the eating and drinking, another prayer of thanksgiving was to be offered.

Chapter 14 of the *Didache* describes a Sunday gathering that included the breaking of bread and thanksgiving. A confession of sins meant to assure the purity of the ritual preceded the gathering.

As Léon-Dufour points out, the Bible is a source of surprise for anyone looking for ready answers about the origin of the Eucharist. The few references to even the most simple eucharistic practices provide a scant defense for those who claim that Christ himself instituted the elaborate eucharistic rituals that developed over time. Moreover, a literal reading of the New Testament does not reveal in detail what Jesus and his followers did when they broke bread. The New Testament accounts, on their own, simply do not provide a clear picture of the Last Supper or of how the early Christians commemorated that event.

Still, if the few references to what Jesus and his first followers did are examined in the broader context of the biblical message and the culture of the times, they can shed light on the beginnings of the Eucharist. These references can then help contemporary Catholics understand what

Mary G. Durkin

Jesus and his followers did. This broader route to examining the Eucharist in the New Testament can also assist contemporary Catholics trying to assess the later controversies surrounding this core sacrament.

What Did Jesus and His Followers Mean by What They Did?

The Bible qualifies as a source for understanding the beginnings of the Eucharist when the question of the meaning of the few eucharistic references is addressed. The actions at the Last Supper are a development, with a significant twist, of ideas and practices that were common in the broader religious and social milieu of the time.

The audiences for the Gospels and Epistles were familiar with these religious and social practices and appreciated the meaning of a ritual meal with bread and a cup of wine. They also knew the meaning, within their cultures, of *body* and *blood,* of *blessing* and *thanksgiving,* of *covenant,* of *sacrifice,* and of *memorial.* Furthermore, since they were familiar with the oral tradition concerning the life and teachings of Jesus, they knew the significance of the ritual practices when used in connection with his memory.

The contemporary reader must consider how Jesus and his followers viewed the various components of both the Last Supper and its commemoration during subsequent gatherings. Even if Jesus, the Twelve, and the early Christians did not articulate a meaning for each gesture and word, they were undoubtedly familiar with the significance attached to what they did and the words they used.

The Eucharist

Both the Last Supper and the breaking of the bread are meal-centered events. In all human cultures, a meal is an event in which the sharing of nourishment can also build family and friendship, community and communication. According to Léon-Dufour, biblical meals signify the unity of those who eat together only if their hearts are in unity. At times, the meal is also an occasion of reconciliation, such as when the Prodigal Son returns or when Jesus eats with his disciples after the resurrection.

The eucharistic meal grew out of the Jewish tradition of a ritual meal, especially the Passover meal with its commemoration of the Exodus and Yahweh's covenant with Israel. That meal recalled Israel's deliverance and anticipated the messianic future where the people would be gathered in a banquet with Yahweh. It strengthened the faith of the Jewish people of Jesus' time.

All Jewish meals with their blessings of food and drink were rooted in the Jewish peoples' memory of themselves as a chosen people. The blessing, or *berakah,* contained a statement of the motive for the blessing. In its formalized version, this blessing was a familiar ritual of table fellowship, acknowledging that everything was from Yahweh who worked wonders for his people. The people, in turn, remembered their relationship to him as well as the responsibilities of that relationship.

Various monastery communities such as the one at Qumran, the site of the Dead Sea Scrolls, also practiced ritual meals that looked forward to a messianic banquet. Their ritual was practiced daily when there were ten or more members present.

Mary G. Durkin

The early Christians were familiar with the ritual meals of traditional Judaism and perhaps with the meals of others who awaited the messianic age. They looked forward, however, to the time in the near future when the Lord would return. Until that time, they would remember Jesus' story when they shared bread and wine. As they shared and remembered, they, too, strengthened their faith.

The Christian ritual meal centers on the bread and the cup of wine. Both bread and wine are responses to the basic human need for nourishment. The bread used in the initial blessing of the Jewish meal represented the blessing of God on the whole meal as well as the fellowship of those taking part in the meal. During Passover, this bread also referred to the bread of affliction in the land of Egypt. In the Christian ritual, the bread and the cup of wine take on added significance because Jesus calls them his body and blood.

To grasp how Jesus' followers interpreted the eating and drinking of his body and blood, it is necessary to understand what body and blood meant to the Jewish community. The anthropology of the New Testament and the nonphilosophical attitude of the New Testament people toward religious mysteries help explain why the early Christians did not share the concerns of later generations over these words and their implications. The early Christians were content with symbolic explanations about how the bread and wine could be "my body" and "my blood of the covenant."

In the institution narratives, the word *body* refers

The Eucharist

to Jesus himself, not just his physical body. The Jewish people did not think people had bodies. Rather, they thought people were their bodies. Eating the body of Jesus would not have connoted the cannibalism of eating the physical body. Rather, the word *body* referred to the person of Jesus. The participants would have known they were being offered the opportunity to share in the very life of Jesus, a life they remembered when they gathered to break bread.

In primitive cultures, *blood* signified life and death situations. The shedding of blood usually meant a loss of vitality. When blood was used in primitive rituals, it often represented either the search for life or the preservation of life.

The ancient Israelites recognized these primitive symbols but, after their experience of the Exodus, gave them new meaning. In Chapter 12 of the Book of Exodus, the Israelites find that sprinkling blood on the doorpost saves the firstborn child. In Chapter 24, at Sinai, Moses sacrifices a bull, sprinkling half the blood on an altar and the other half on the people. This cultic act was a sign of the covenant between Yahweh and the people. In the rituals of the Jewish community, blood came to stand for what Yahweh had done for the community. It, too, reminded them of their part in the covenant with him.

As Jews, Jesus and his followers were familiar with this meaning of blood in the context of their covenant with Yahweh. Indeed, Jesus' words, "This is my blood of the covenant," parallel the words of Moses, "This is the blood of the covenant." Léon-Dufour sees the words *body/*

Mary G. Durkin

blood standing for *person/covenant of God in my blood.*

Michael Lawler in *Symbol and Sacrament* argues that the use of the word *blood* at the Last Supper refers to Jesus in his whole person. The Jesus that is remembered in the Eucharist is the Jesus "given-for-you and poured-out-for-you." This Jesus, Lawler maintains, is the one sacrificed, crucified, and raised from the dead. By these actions, Jesus established the covenant sought after in all sacrifices. Thus, the idea of the Eucharist as sacrifice is linked to Jesus' words concerning his body and blood and the covenant.

The meaning of the Eucharist as sacrifice became the subject of much debate in later centuries. For this reason, it is helpful to try to understand what the idea of sacrifice first meant within the culture of the New Testament. The most important feature of the worship of ancient Israel was sacrifice. The Books of Exodus, Leviticus, and Numbers contain extensive instructions about sacrifice. Later Old Testament writings refer more specifically to various sacrificial practices.

Three types of sacrifice appear in the Old Testament, all undoubtedly related, in some way, to the practices of other primitive cultures. The first type is the communion sacrifice in which the faithful share a feast with the gods. The second is the whole burnt offering, a sacrifice common for atonement and thanksgiving, offered as a tribute to a god. The third is a sin offering, a gift offering intended to cleanse the sanctuary of impurities. The blood of the sin offering was used to cleanse the sanctuary. Private sin offerings were necessary if one failed to cleanse oneself after

The Eucharist

the period of impurity had passed. In addition, the Passover ritual and the Day of Atonement ritual (in which an animal bears everyone's sins) were sacrificial rituals for the Jewish people. The Passover ritual was closely related to the communion sacrifice and undoubtedly influenced the early Christian interpretation of the Last Supper.

The idea of sacrifice, of an offering in acknowledgement of God's lordship and his people's dependence, remained an important element of religious practice at the time of Jesus. Thus, it is not surprising that the early Christians came to see his crucifixion as a sacrificial death. The Lord's Supper commemorated his death as well as his resurrection. The institution narratives recounted the story of a sacrificial meal in which blood was poured out for others for the forgiveness of their sins and a new covenant was sealed in blood.

The Epistle to the Hebrews suggested that Christ was both priest and victim. The author maintained that the contrast between Christ and other Jewish and pagan priests was obvious. Those priests continually repeated the same sacrifices, which never took away sins. Christ offered a single sacrifice for sins and then sat down at the right hand of God. His one sacrifice was all that was needed for forgiveness.

In Ephesians 5:2, Paul advises his listeners to walk in love as Christ did when he gave himself up as a fragrant offering and a sacrifice to God. When Jesus' disciples followed his instructions and did what he had done—in his memory—they, too, were able to walk in love, thanks to his one sacrifice.

Mary G. Durkin

Remembering what Jesus did at the Last Supper, crucifixion, and resurrection made their gatherings memorial rituals. Like the memorial ritual of the Passover, the rite was an *anamnesis,* an objective memorial in which the remembering brought to life the divine occurrence it remembered. In the Old Testament, remembering, as at Passover time, had a threefold objective: an event was remembered for what happened in the past, its effect on the present, and the hope it engendered for the future. The effects in the present and the hope for the future were possible because of the divine activity remembered.

In summary, the New Testament roots of the Eucharist point to it as a ritual memorial meal celebrated by those who believed they were to do as Jesus directed them at the Last Supper. For Jesus' early followers, the ritual of gathering and breaking of bread had meaning because it let them experience Jesus' presence even after he was no longer physically present in their midst. They understood his reference to his body and blood as a sign of their participation in him through his sacrifice. This sacrifice purified them so that they could once again respond to the covenant God offered.

Within the context of the Good News that was preached by Jesus, the teachings of his ministry, and the interpretation of his message in the Epistles and Gospels, this meal also helped the early Christians understand how they were to continue his memory by the way they lived. As St. Paul made clear to the Corinthians, Christians were one body. Separating into factions and lacking concern for those less fortunate disturbed the unity they were to proclaim.

The Eucharist

As the early Christians made the absent one present, they deepened their own appreciation of the salvation he brought with his Good News. They anticipated the day that they would drink the new wine with him in the kingdom of the Father.

CHAPTER FOUR

From Fellowship Meal to Private Worship

AFTER reviewing the beginnings of the Eucharist recorded in the New Testament, a contemporary Catholic might wonder how the Church moved from the ideas and practices of the Apostolic era to the pre-Vatican II understanding of the Eucharist. The elaborate liturgical practices of the pre-Vatican II Mass are a far cry from the simple fellowship meal of the New Testament.

If, as some scholars maintain, the New Testament institution narratives reflect a eucharistic celebration at the end of a fellowship meal, then how does that practice relate to the highly clerical, nonparticipatory ritual of the Tridentine Sacrifice of the Mass developed as a result of the Council of Trent? How could the Church claim that Christ instituted the Eucharist as it was celebrated in the first half of the twentieth century?

Unlike many Protestant churches, the Catholic Church does not claim that the Scriptures alone support its teachings. The authority for its doctrinal pronouncements rests in Scripture *and* Tradition. Thus, contemporary Catholic eucharistic theology and liturgy must consider the tradition of the Eucharist as well as its origins in the Bible. Catholics

The Eucharist

study both these sources when searching for a valid correlation between the sacrament and contemporary human experience.

Eucharistic practices and theological interpretations of these practices evolved through the centuries and were often influenced by the culture of the times. Theological reflection, eucharistic practice, and the laity's eucharistic piety all reflect how each age reacted to the mystery of this core sacramental experience.

Catholic scholars must assess these past developments when trying to determine what constitutes a valid contemporary treatment of the Eucharist. They must decide which developments reflect a legitimate response to Jesus' command "do this in memory of me." They also must uncover which developments, dictated by cultures of different times, are nonessential for a valid contemporary theology.

A development might be judged nonessential because it was dictated more by the secular practices or problems of an era than by a search for a legitimate response to Christ's command. Although a practice or interpretation might have been valid at the time it first appeared, new insights into the original eucharistic practices might suggest that its focus would be inappropriate today. Furthermore, many of these nonessential developments, while valid for their times, do not speak to contemporary experience.

From the very beginning of Christianity, the Eucharist has been the core expression of the meaning of Christian life and membership in the Christian community. It has been *the* sacrament. Understandably, then, the development of the Eucharist reflects how individuals and the

Mary G. Durkin

Christian community have viewed themselves through the ages.

When interpreting the Eucharist, scholars from each period have addressed a variety of issues. Reviewing their extensive writings on the Eucharist, a contemporary Catholic can uncover three key themes that have appeared with varying emphasis throughout the history of the Church. Themes of Sacrifice, the Real Presence, and Unity emerge in one form or another in the eucharistic discussions of each period.

Catholics can survey the eucharistic practices of the Patristic era, the Middle Ages, and the Reformation/Trent period to learn how each historic culture contributed to the development of the pre-Vatican II Mass. A review of the key themes as they emerged during the same periods will show how the meaning of this sacrament evolved as well. This analysis also will help explain how changes in eucharistic practices and theology following Vatican II do not attack, as Lefebvre claims, the essential truths of the Catholic faith.

Patristic Period

During the four to five centuries following the Apostolic era, the Eucharist developed from a simple ritual celebrated in the home to an elaborate ritual celebrated in the splendor of the basilica. The practices of the imperial court, rather than those of the Jewish ritual meal, began to be the model for the ritual. In most instances, eucharistic

The Eucharist

theology grew out of these liturgical practices, which often were responses to outside challenges to Christian beliefs. The differences between practices and interpretations of the earlier and later years of the Patristic era are extensive enough to warrant looking at each separately.

Early Patristic Practices

Various sources provide information on the practices of the early post-Apostolic period. From writings of the time, it is clear that, as Christianity spread, different practices developed in different places. Cultural distinctions as well as personal preferences of leaders influenced the way the Eucharist came to be celebrated in different areas. Excerpts from writings of the early Fathers of the Church, as well as from some secular observers, describe the eucharistic practices of the period.

The developing eucharistic ritual bore the marks of the changed expectations of the Christian community—a factor that repeats itself over and over through the ages. As early as the second century, two acclamations were no longer being used. Both *"Maranatha"* ("Come, Lord, come") and "May the grace of Christ come and the world pass away" were expressions that looked to the imminent return of the Lord. Once it became obvious that this expectation was not likely to be met, the acclamations were dropped.

There is early evidence of a Christian Sunday morning prayer service modeled on the Sabbath service. This ser-

Mary G. Durkin

vice included the greeting by the presider, "The Lord be with you," and the response "And with your spirit." This exchange was followed by scripture readings, a sermon, prayers of petition, and a formal dismissal.

Sometimes, a Eucharist immediately followed this service. Other times, the Eucharist took place in the evening. By the middle of the second century, the separation of the Eucharist from the fellowship meal occurred in some places but not in others. Still, by the year 200, most communities held the meal only on special occasions.

Perhaps abuses, similar to those Paul observed in Corinth, led them to drop the meal. They also may have separated the meal from the eucharistic ritual when increased membership in the community made it difficult for all to join in the traditional fellowship meal.

Ignatius (who died around 110) was the second bishop of Antioch and an important pastor of the post-Apostolic period. He wrote letters to other churches in which he referred to Sunday as the Sabbath day for Christians. He also observed that only a bishop could preside over the Eucharist. The bishop alone said the words of thanksgiving. While there was an office of priest at this time, the priest's role was to assist the bishop, preparing the offerings and breaking and distributing bread. The priest could preside only if appointed by a bishop.

According to the testimony of Pliny the Younger of Bythinia in Asia Minor, the Christians held two meetings on a fixed day of the week. In the year 112, he wrote his superiors seeking advice on how to deal with the Christians. He reported that they met before dawn on a fixed day. At

The Eucharist

these early morning meetings, they sang a hymn to their god, Christ, and took an oath to do no wrong. Later that same day, they met again for a religious meal.

Justin Martyr, who converted to Christianity around 130, wrote two defenses of the faith, *Apologies* and *Dialogue with Trypho*. Both shed light on early eucharistic practices. He described a eucharistic celebration that took place on Sundays, with a service modelled on the synagogue ritual. He said Christians gathered on Sunday because on Sunday God created the world and Jesus Christ rose from the dead.

The form of the Sunday ritual which he described was probably used in most Western churches by the middle of the second century. It included readings from the memoirs of the apostles or from the writings of the prophets; an address by the presider of the meeting; prayers of intercession by all present; a kiss of peace; a long prayer of praise and thanksgiving with no set form but which included the words of institution and was proclaimed by the presider; an "Amen" by the congregation; and a communion in which all—celebrant, deacon, and people—received the bread and the wine that was mixed with water.

A portion of the bread was reserved for those who were not able to be present and was brought to them after the gathering. In addition, the wealthy made contributions that the presider then distributed to those in need.

Justin also wrote about a yearly Eucharist service held after the initiation of new Christians. At this service, there were common prayers, followed by a kiss of peace. The people then offered the presider bread and a cup of wine

Mary G. Durkin

mixed with water. He offered a prayer glorifying the Father of the universe through the name of the Son and the Holy Spirit. The people answered, "Amen." The deacons then distributed to all the bread and the wine and water over which the thanksgiving had been said. The bread and cup also were carried to those who were absent.

The Teaching of the Twelve Apostles, written in Syria in the middle of the second century, contains another record of a eucharistic practice from this era. This source includes a eucharistic prayer but makes no reference to the words of institution. It does refer to the community's weekly meal as a sacrifice, however.

A third-century record of eucharistic practice is found in *The Apostolic Tradition* by Hippolytus of Rome. Written about 215, this liturgical book outlined the order of service for the consecration of a bishop and for the initiation of the catechumens. A communion service followed both rituals, and it conformed to the pattern outlined by Justin. Hippolytus also included examples of prayers that might be used during the service. Presiding bishops, however, were not to memorize these prayers, only to use them as examples.

During that same period, Tertullian wrote that Christians met for the Eucharist before dawn on days other than Sunday. He noted that some members of the community took the bread home to eat before their own meals. Later in the third century, Cyprian of Carthage described how Christians met daily in small groups for the Eucharist, sometimes holding these meetings in conjunction with an evening meal.

The Eucharist

These practices of the first three centuries show that the Eucharist continued as a symbolic, festive meal patterned after the Jewish thanksgiving prayer service but with no set words save for the words of institution. Though there were differences in different places, a basic pattern seemed to prevail by the end of the third century.

This pattern included the offering of bread and wine and the thanksgiving (Eucharist) prayer over the gifts by the leader of the community, with additional prayers directed to God the Father in thanksgiving for the gifts received, especially for the redemption brought by Christ. The Eucharists of the period also included the breaking of bread and the sharing of the bread and the cup of wine mixed with water. The entire ritual action was seen as making the bread and the wine sacred.

Furthermore, the worship was always that of the community. The leaders prayed with the members but not for them.

Early Patristic Interpretations

The early Fathers of the Church picked up on New Testament references to the Eucharist as sacrifice, to the bread and cup of wine as the body and blood of Christ, and to the Eucharist as a source of unity. Later scholars base their discussions of sacrifice and of the Real Presence on ideas from this period. The early Fathers, however, did not share all the concerns of later interpreters. They were responding to particular challenges of their own culture.

Mary G. Durkin

Thus, it is important to understand the contexts of these terms and to consider that the early Fathers may not have been as explicit in their definitions as later scholars took them to be.

The early Fathers based the idea of the Eucharist as sacrifice on the New Testament accounts of the institution narratives and on Paul's teachings that Christ was a sacrifice to God. In addition, their references to the Eucharist as a sacrifice or a sacrificial meal were often in reaction to charges that the Christians were atheists who offered no sacrifice.

Early in the second century, Ignatius called the Christian meeting place a place of sacrifice. Justin referred to the Eucharist as the sacrifice of the Church and called the contributions of the people an offering. Referring to Malachi's prophecy that in every place a pure sacrifice will be offered to God, Ignatius stated that the sacrifices commanded by Christ and offered in every place by Christians were pleasing to God.

In the beginning of the third century, Irenaeus described the Christians as a priestly people who offered a new covenant sacrifice. He, too, referred to Malachi when declaring the Christian Eucharist to be the sacrifice that glorified God's name among all nations.

Tertullian described the Eucharist as an offering and a sacrifice. Cyprian said both the leader and the people offered the sacrifice but Christ was the real priest. He saw the Last Supper and the Eucharist as representations of Christ's sacrifice on the cross. In Cyprian's view, both the

The Eucharist

offering and the sacrifice of the people must be a response to Christ's Passion.

On the issue of the Real Presence, the early Fathers supported the biblical claim that the bread and the cup of wine and water became the body and the blood of Christ. They did not attempt to explain *how* this happened, being content to assert that it did happen.

Clement of Alexandria, a Father of the East, described the Eucharist as a sacrifice and as the food for believers. He distinguished between Christ's human blood and his eucharistic, spiritual blood. The blood of Christ's flesh redeems people from their corruption while the spiritual blood anoints them. To drink the blood of Christ makes one a partaker in his immortality. As the wine is blended with the water, the Spirit, the energetic principle of the Word of God, is blended with the believer. The mixture of wine and water nourishes faith, and the Spirit leads to immortality. This mixture of the drink and the Word he calls Eucharist, a "renowned and glorious grace; and they who by faith partake of it are sanctified in body and soul."

St. Ignatius of Antioch said that the Eucharist was the flesh and blood of the Savior, who the Father raised from the dead. He accused the Docetist heretics of abstaining from the Eucharist because they did not confess that the Eucharist was the flesh of Jesus Christ who suffered for sins and whom the Father raised by his goodness. He also maintained that he desired the "bread of God," which was the flesh of Jesus as well as his blood.

Justin Martyr taught that the food that has been made

Mary G. Durkin

Eucharist is the flesh and blood of Jesus who was made incarnate through the Word of God for human salvation. He believed that the flesh and blood of the Eucharist nourished and transformed the flesh and blood of those who received the Eucharist.

In the early part of the third century, St. Irenaeus declared that, after the invocation, the bread was no longer common bread but the Eucharist, the body and blood of Christ. The bread was the body of the Lord and the cup of wine was his blood. The Gnostic disparagement of earthly substances was invalid according to his theology of the Eucharist. Against the Gnostic heretics, therefore, he maintained that this Eucharist had both an earthly and heavenly reality.

Later in the century, Cyprian justified the practice of permitting those persecuted Christians who repented after denying their faith to receive the Eucharist again. He felt that if they were to be asked to shed their blood for Christ, they should also be permitted to share in his blood.

In addition to eucharistic themes of sacrifice and the Real Presence, the early Fathers developed the concept of the Eucharist as an expression and basis of Christian unity. All three themes were rooted in New Testament beginnings. When the Fathers reflected on the Eucharist as a sign of unity, however, they were undoubtedly influenced by the fellowship ritual of the Apostolic age as well as by St. Paul's emphasis on the unity necessary for proper participation in the breaking of the bread.

St. Ignatius of Antioch believed that having one bishop preside at the Eucharist was a sign of the one Eucharist

The Eucharist

consisting of the one flesh of Christ. The thanksgiving prayer of Hippolytus beseeches God to send the Holy Spirit on the offering of the Church to bring together in unity all who receive it. Both Pope Clement of Rome and Polycarp, also writing in the second century, viewed the Eucharist, presided over by a bishop, as a sign of unity.

In the third century, Cyprian argued that when the Lord called the bread, which was made of many different grains, his "body," he meant that all the Christian people he bears in his heart must be united. So, too, when he called the cup of wine, made from many grapes, his "blood," he meant that the flock formed by those partaking of it should be one community.

Some scholars maintain that the previous themes of sacrifice and the Real Presence were important to the Fathers because of their desire to emphasize the unity brought by Christ. These three themes were woven together in the New Testament texts and continued to be seen as interdependent in the eucharistic interpretations of the early Fathers.

Later Patristic Practices

From the fourth to the sixth centuries, eucharistic practices changed greatly. The short, simple ritual meal begun in Apostolic times and continued in the second and third centuries evolved into an elaborate ceremony.

During the fourth century, Christianity responded to its new, public status. Beginning with Constantine's lifting of the ban against Christian worship in 313 and continuing

Mary G. Durkin

through Theodosius' proclamation of Christianity as the official state religion in 380, the Christian religion underwent major cultural changes. The Church moved from being a persecuted entity to a state religion. The resultant adjustment in the Church's self-understanding could be seen in the way it celebrated its core sacrament of the Eucharist. Both liturgical practices and theological interpretations responded to the Church's new status.

One example of that response can be found in the changing role of the bishop. Constantine appointed the bishops to perform certain civil functions and gave them the secular symbols of their civil roles. As a result, in both eucharistic gatherings and the secular world, the character of the bishop underwent a major change that would have longlasting repercussions.

As judges, bishops began to wear special attire. They acquired rings and thrones in the execution of their public office. These accoutrements, along with the various incensings, torches, and genuflections offered to judges, became accepted trappings of the bishop's office. After the fall of the empire, these special symbols became a sign of the bishop's position. Many of them continue to be used today.

Moving the place of public worship from a simple liturgical setting in a house or meeting hall to the elaborate environment of the basilica added to the pomp surrounding the Eucharist. The increased number of Christians required larger meeting places. It was only natural for Constantine, who built the first basilica, to borrow the building

The Eucharist

design from places used for state functions. The style of the basilica, a rectangular building with a raised stage at one end, soon became the dominant style of Church buildings. Finally, in the fifth century, when the bishop's church could no longer accommodate everyone, permission was given to priests to celebrate Mass for those who could not be present at the bishop's celebration.

Christianity's changed status in the empire also resulted in the lengthening of the liturgies. Once Sunday became an official day of rest in 321, Christians developed liturgies of two to four hours. Longer prayers were added to existing liturgies and included references to events in the Old Testament, the life of Christ, and Church history. Prayers of petition, covering the many needs of both religious and civic life, also increased. The recitation of the Our Father before communion became a common practice toward the end of the fourth century.

Bishops continued to improvise the eucharistic prayers, although they followed the general outline of praise and thanksgiving found in Jewish services. Some bishops began writing their prayers for others to imitate and, in some places, even included the rubrics of the liturgy. In the fifth century, Popes St. Leo and Gelesius initiated a form of standardization of liturgical ritual which future popes would make mandatory.

Feast day eucharistic celebrations, in addition to Easter and Pentecost, proliferated. The Eucharist began to be celebrated on Christmas, the Epiphany, the Ascension, and the feasts of the apostles and early martyrs. By the end

Mary G. Durkin

of the fourth century, Mass was celebrated every day in some places, though these Masses were not as well attended as the Sunday liturgies.

St. Basil, writing during this time, claimed that he received communion four times a week: on Sunday, Wednesday, Friday, and Saturday. He encouraged others to "communicate every day and to partake of the holy body and blood of Christ."

Different practices of the Eastern and Western churches which are still evident today had their origin as far back as this period. Jerusalem, Antioch, and Constantinople were the liturgical centers of the East. In the fourth century, Church Fathers like Basil and John Chrysostom developed elaborate liturgies. Since this period, there has been little substantive change in the eucharistic celebrations of the Eastern churches.

In the East, the short penitential rituals that took place before the Eucharist became, by the fourth century, litanies ending with "Lord, have mercy," a practice not taken up by the West until the fifth century. The East chose to replace the festival of the Egyptian sun god, Osiris, on January 6 with a feast honoring the birth of Christ. The West, however, celebrated Christmas on December 25, the Roman festival of the birth of the sun.

Near the end of the fourth century, Greek ceased to be the common language of the people. The Eastern churches then translated their liturgies into the native languages of the different Eastern congregations. The Western liturgies turned to Latin as the official language.

Around the same time, in the Western church, the word

The Eucharist

Mass (*missa*), a shortened version of *missarum solemnia,* became the popular name for the eucharistic celebration. *Missa* referred to the words used when the catechumens were dismissed prior to the offering of gifts and to the dismissal of the entire congregation at the conclusion of the celebration.

Despite the various changes in liturgical practices throughout this period, the Roman Masses of the fourth and fifth century were still community-centered, with the altar a table. By the end of the sixth century, however, the Roman liturgy adopted the elaborate style of the East. The result was a clerical-centered liturgy with some lay participation. The size of the congregation and the basilica turned the Eucharist into a ritual event that one attended and watched as opposed to a ritual meal in which one participated. Still, the eucharistic celebrations of the later Patristic period continued to have a communal flavor. Even in the basilica, there was only one altar at which only one celebration took place.

Later Patristic Interpretations

The issues of sacrifice, the Real Presence, and the Eucharist as a source of unity continued to be addressed by the later Church Fathers. As in the earlier Patristic period, however, the ongoing discussion was not, for the most part, theoretical. Even when the Fathers discussed the Eucharist in response to the Arian heresy's denial of the divinity of Christ, they did not engage in deep philosophi-

Mary G. Durkin

cal analysis. Nevertheless, their writings reveal how the Eucharist expressed their understanding of the meaning of Christ for their time.

The idea of the Eucharist as a sacrifice was accepted by this time, although no clear-cut meaning was assigned to the idea of sacrifice. St. Cyril of Jerusalem in the fourth century referred to the "spiritual sacrifice, the unbloody worship" in which the victim is offered in propitiation to appease God. After this spiritual sacrifice, the participants pray for all those in need of help, convinced that their prayers rise up in the presence of Christ.

St. Augustine declared that Christ, the great High Priest, offered himself to God through his Passion. Christ made this sacrifice so "we might be members of this glorious head." This sacrifice is also the one celebrated in the Eucharist. In celebrating the Eucharist, the Church teaches that she herself is offered and Christ is both the Priest who offers and the sacrifice offered.

Emphasizing the sacrificial nature of the Eucharist led, during this period, to less frequent reception of communion. If the bishop offered the sacrifice on behalf of the people, it no longer seemed necessary for the other participants to partake of the Eucharist.

As the Eucharist came to be seen as an atonement offering for sin, Christ became both victim and priest. Some writers declared that the Eucharist was a symbolic representation of Christ's Passion. Christ as Priest became associated with the actions of the bishop. Christ as Victim was associated with the bread and wine that were offered and destroyed. Therefore, Christ's role became passive as well.

The Eucharist

The victim was offered by the Church to God the Father. Again, in this period, there was little detailed theoretical discussion of the Real Presence. The Fathers acknowledged that what seemed to be bread and wine was actually the body and blood of Christ and that this change took place by the powerful Word of God. The precise manner of change did not seem to be a major point of argument.

Augustine claimed that the bread—once sanctified by the Word of God—was the body of Christ and the contents of the chalice—once sanctified—were the blood.

In response to Arianism, however, the Fathers emphasized Christ's presence in the body and blood by focusing on his presence as God. The prayers that formerly were addressed to God the Father now were addressed to Christ or to the Trinity. Father, Son, and Holy Spirit were all on the same level. This emphasis on the Eucharist as the body and blood of God also led to less frequent reception of communion. The elements of communion were seen as sacred, removed from the people.

Theologians did debate when Christ became present in the body and blood. Earlier, it had been thought that Christ was present during the entire short eucharistic service. Then, when a prayer service began to precede the eucharistic service, Christ came to be seen as present just in the eucharistic prayer—beginning with the offering of the bread and wine and ending with the reception of the body and blood of Christ.

With the later split between the Eastern and Western churches, their differences on this point became more apparent. Though both churches thought the bread and wine

Mary G. Durkin

were the body and blood of Christ, who was mystically present, they disagreed on the moment Christ became present. Ambrose of Milan supported the Western position. He argued that the words of institution were the words of consecration. Cyril of Jerusalem, however, held the prevailing Eastern view. For him, it was the calling down of the Holy Spirit on the bread and wine that turned them into the body and blood of Christ.

He claimed that this body and blood of Christ were, in turn, responsible for the unity of those who participated in the Eucharist. According to Cyril, it was through his one body that Christ sanctified the faithful in the mystical communion, making them one body with him and among themselves. St. Augustine maintained that to say "Amen" to "The body of Christ," recipients first must be members of the body of Christ. Otherwise, their "Amen" would be untrue. Following St. Paul, he also taught that if the recipients were the body of Christ and also his members, they placed their own mystery on the altar and then received it.

Middle Ages

Practices

By the beginning of the sixth century, the basic format of the Mass had been established. Cultural influences, however, continued to lead to changes that affected the way Western Christians celebrated the Eucharist.

Records of eucharistic practices of the sixth and seventh centuries indicate that the celebration of the Eucharist con-

The Eucharist

tinued to be shaped by its original Jewish/New Testament roots. Eucharistic practices also reflected Greek traditions, however, and began to assimilate more traditions of the imperial court. Even in modified form, the continued use of Jewish scripture readings, the thanksgiving and praise of the Canon, and the doxologies maintained the connection between the Eucharist and an Old Testament ritual meal. Exorcisms, anointings, night baptisms, and many of the words associated with sacrament—*liturgy, Eucharist,* and *mystery,* for example—are Greek in origin. The position of subdeacon, the introduction of the chasuble, and the ritual entrance procession all followed the model of the imperial court.

By the ninth century, a style had developed in Northern Europe which combined both Roman and Celtic influences with those of the East. The result was a liturgy combining long, repetitious prayers with longer periods of silent prayers by the celebrant, who made many signs of the cross during the Canon. Frequent declarations of unworthiness, along with multiple incensings of the sacred objects, reflected the prevailing awe and fear of the Eucharist.

Pope Gelesius had introduced a common liturgical book in 500. By the time of Gregory the Great in the seventh century, standardization of the liturgy became the norm. The Roman titular churches, however, were still allowed to use their own books, providing for some diversity. Then, in the eleventh century, the Pope demanded that all Western churches follow the customs of Rome. Only Milan, despite numerous papal edicts, refused the directive and continued to use the rite of St. Ambrose.

Mary G. Durkin

Latin was used in liturgies throughout the West, but it was understood only by the clergy and the small proportion of the laity who were educated. The prayers of the Eucharist were spoken in Latin, furthering the idea that the sacrament was a sacred "secret." The priest no longer celebrated the Eucharist with the people. Rather, he now said Mass for the congregation.

The priest's role took on increased significance with the introduction of the private Mass. This practice began in the monasteries where many monks became priests. These Masses developed into silent exercises because many priests celebrated at once, often at the same altar or altars close to one another. By the end of Middle Ages, every priest was obligated to celebrate Mass every day.

The votive Mass, offered for a special intention, reflected how the understanding of the Eucharist changed during this period. Instead of being offered for the whole Church, the Mass was addressed to the needs of a specific group or person. According to this view, the Mass functioned as a mechanical source of grace. Flagrant abuses accompanied the offering of stipends for these votive Masses, however, and eventually led to the calls for reform.

The church architecture of the Middle Ages also contributed to the loss of a communal sense of celebration. The altar was attached to the rear wall, separated from the congregation by the choir and, at times, a screen.

During the same period, reverence for the sacred elements of the Eucharist increased. Practices centered on the Real Presence in the consecrated host. The practice of re-

The Eucharist

ceiving communion in the hand ended, and the priest began distributing communion to people kneeling at the altar rail, which separated them from the priest and the altar during the Mass. In the eleventh century, genuflections before the sacred elements became common. In the twelfth century, a sanctuary lamp signaled the presence of the body of Christ in the Church. In the thirteenth century, the elevation of the host was introduced, and the cup was no longer offered to the congregation. These practices reflected the belief that the Eucharist was so holy that only holy people could be associated with it. Thus, the Eucharist was the work of the priest. Priesthood came to be understood in terms of the priest's power to consecrate.

The resulting sense of unworthiness on the part of the laity led to a further decrease in the reception of communion. Many of the great saints of the twelfth, thirteenth, fourteenth, and fifteenth centuries did not receive communion regularly. In one recorded instance, special permission from Rome was requested for daily communion.

St. Francis encouraged devotion to the Eucharist, but this devotion did not extend to reception of communion. In 1253, the Pope approved the rule for an order founded by St. Clare. This rule allowed members of the order to receive communion seven times a year. Attempting to combat this false sense of unworthiness, the Fourth Lateran Council in 1215 made it obligatory for Catholics to receive communion at least once a year.

In general, however, the eucharistic practices of the Middle Ages moved the Eucharist far from its New Testament roots. Eventually, standardization of prayers and

Mary G. Durkin

rubrics prevailed. A cult of the sacred elements led to less reception of communion. Private or votive Masses, often said for stipends, became common. Over this period of seven or eight centuries, the Eucharist became less and less the community-centered memorial meal of its origins.

Interpretations

Though the theologians of the Middle Ages did not ignore the issues of sacrifice and unity, they focused primarily on the idea of the Real Presence and on how it occurred. The concept of transubstantiation came to the forefront during this period.

Berengar of Tours, whose work led to the definition of a sacrament in the eleventh century, denied that there were changes in the substance of the bread and wine in the Eucharist. He did not think that the body of Christ was corporeally present on the altar after the words of consecration. He argued that Christ could not appear again before the Last Judgment. Because of his beliefs, however, Berengar became the center of an ongoing controversy and was chastised by a series of popes. Finally, in 1079, Pope Gregory VII ordered him to take an oath affirming that the Christ in the Eucharist was the Christ of history.

Peter of Caupa claimed that the various and, at times, conflicting theories about how the bread and wine became the body and blood of Christ made at least one point clear: it is more important to believe that the body of Christ is present on the altar at the solemn words than to know how this conversion takes place. The change, as Peter asserted,

The Eucharist

is a mystery. Peter's position was not unlike that of the Patristic Fathers, who were content to affirm that each substance (the bread and wine) became another (the body and blood). The Greeks of the fourth and fifth centuries had not been as content, however. They had searched for an explanation, struggling with words like *conversion, transference,* and *transformation* to explain the change that they acknowledged took place. It is not surprising, then, that scholars in the medieval climate of intellectual pursuit also sought a philosophical explanation to clarify the mystery. The word that seemed most effective for their purposes was *transubstantiation.* By this term, scholars meant that the substance (the reality) of the elements changed even though their appearance remained as bread and wine.

Modern scholars trace the first use of the word *transubstantiate* to Rolando Bandinelli (Pope Alexander III) in 1140. The word *transubstantiation* first appeared in a twelfth-century text of Stephen of Autun. From the middle of the twelfth century, it began to appear frequently. In the early thirteenth century, Hildebert of Tours taught that the bread and wine were transubstantiated into the body and the blood of Christ.

The Fourth Lateran Council of 1215 used Hildebert's teaching in its pronouncement on the Eucharist. The Council decreed that the body and blood of Jesus Christ are "truly contained in the sacrament of the altar under the species of bread and wine; the bread (changed) into his body by divine power of transubstantiation and the wine into his blood." This transubstantiation occurs, according

Mary G. Durkin

to the Council statement, "to accomplish the mystery of unity we ourselves receive from his (nature) and what he himself received from ours." Even with this pronouncement, however, the theory of transubstantiation was not looked upon as Church doctrine.

Later in the century, the Scholastics, especially Thomas Aquinas, gave this theory enough philosophical underpinnings to satisfy future scholars. Aquinas argued that God, who is infinite act, is able to cause conversion of both form and reality "so that the whole substance of *this* is converted into the whole substance of *that*." (Italics added.) In the Eucharist, he believed, divine power converts the whole substance of bread and wine into the whole substance of the body and blood of Christ through transubstantiation rather than through natural motion. Aquinas maintained that the resultant conversion is not formal but substantial. Christ's Real Presence in the Eucharist is a supernatural and metaphysical presence that is visible through faith.

With the other great Scholastics, Aquinas denied that annihilation is the means of this conversion. He also rejected the idea that some change takes place in the body of Christ during this conversion.

Aquinas' theology of the Eucharist is extensive. On the subject of unity, he first declared that the purpose of the Eucharist is to nourish Christians. As food, the Eucharist communicates divine life to its recipients. Those who receive the Eucharist are then united with Christ, which in turn unites them with the Church, his body on earth.

Aquinas' theory on the sacrifice of the Mass also con-

The Eucharist

tributed to new understandings of the Eucharist and the Mass. His ideas provided the framework for later theories separating a theology of the Eucharist from a theology of the Sacrifice of the Mass.

Scholars disagree, however, on whether this theoretical separation is based on an accurate interpretation of Aquinas' teaching. Some claim that a correct reading of Aquinas shows him believing that sacrament and sacrifice are one, the Mass being the sacrament celebrated. According to others, Aquinas and the Scholastics believed that the Mass was a sacred action in which sacred objects were produced, but the Eucharist was only the sacred objects. From this perspective, the Eucharist is different from other sacraments, which are sacred actions. Aquinas also argued that the Mass was not a distinct sacrifice but a commemoration of Christ's sacrifice on Calvary.

In keeping with his teaching on the cause and effect of sacraments, Thomas held that the Eucharist was only effective if those who participated or those for whom the Mass was offered cooperated with God's grace. Only the consecration of the elements occurred automatically. By virtue of his priesthood, the celebrant had the power to change the bread and wine into the body and blood. The disposition of the priest, therefore, did not affect the validity of the sacrament.

Reformation/Counter-Reformation

Despite this flowering of eucharistic theology under the Scholastics, the eucharistic practices of the Middle Ages

Mary G. Durkin

eventually led to a deteriorating appreciation for the origins of this core sacrament. As the catalogue of abuses increased, attempts at reform became inevitable. Some attempts took place within the Church. By the beginning of the sixteenth century, however, people citing dissatisfaction with the Mass called for a reform movement separate from the Church. Thus, the Protestant Reformation came into being.

Contemporary scholars debate whether it was simply abuses that led to the reformers' departure from the Church or if there were fundamental differences in the theologies of the reformers and the theology that served as the basis for the Church's response at the Council of Trent. Since there was no unified understanding of the Eucharist among the reformers, a variety of practices and theories flourished.

Practices

The Reformers criticized many abuses, including the following practices related to the Eucharist: superstitious rituals; the celebration of other Masses during the Solemn Mass; Masses with no one assisting; Masses with no one, not even the priest, receiving communion; brawls between groups from different churches during Blessed Sacrament processions; indecent celebrations with profane songs and drinking bouts; and excessive numbers of low Masses said for stipends by avaricious priests. The Reformers attributed all these abuses to the Church's misunderstanding of the Eucharist and to the Scholastic notion of a priest offer-

The Eucharist

ing the sacrifice of the Mass for others. To correct these abuses, the Reformers developed their own worship services. They wished to model their worship on the biblical Last Supper, so they discarded the word Mass and used the designation "The Lord's Supper" or, in some instances "The Lord's Table."

In 1523, Luther designed a new Latin service. He followed this with a German version in 1526. He wanted to eliminate any association between his service and the concept of the Eucharist as sacrifice and therefore dispensed with the Offertory and the Canon. The priest pronounced the words of consecration which were found in Paul's Letter to the Corinthians. Luther also condemned the practices of reserving and venerating the Eucharist. Because he believed that all Christians were priests, he wanted everyone participating in worship to partake of the chalice.

Calvin, who rejected the Catholic understanding of priest, created two services to replace the Mass. One consisted of scripture readings and a sermon. The other was a service for the distribution of communion.

The Anglicans originally kept the Mass, though in 1547 Parliament accepted a bill that authorized communion under both species. This declaration led the Anglican Church to insert a new Order of Communion into the Latin Mass.

Interpretations: The Reformers

To understand why the Reformers changed the worship services, it is necessary to consider their different eucharistic theologies. As with their overall approach to the sacra-

Mary G. Durkin

ments, they had no uniform theology of the Eucharist. Yet their various eucharistic theologies demonstrate how the Eucharist reflects the core beliefs of a Christian church. The positions of Luther and Calvin represent several areas in which the Reformers disagreed with the Catholic Church's teachings on the Eucharist and, indirectly, with the Church's understanding of the Christian community.

Luther attacked the Mass, often using harsh language because he saw the Mass as the cornerstone of Catholicism. The idea that the Mass could be both a good work and a sacrifice did not fit his understanding of Christ's words. He rejected the idea of any human mediation between God and sinner, be it through the Mass or the Church. Although he accepted Christ's presence in the Eucharist, he limited it to the moments of consecration and communion.

He also rejected the idea of transubstantiation, finding no basis for it in Scripture. He thought the term meant that the reality of the bread and wine vanished and his senses could not agree with that. He maintained that this invention of St. Thomas Aquinas was valid only because the Church claimed it was. Rejecting the power of the Church to make this determination, he proposed the theory of consubstantiation. He meant that both bread and wine and the body and blood of Christ were substantially present in the sacrament.

Calvin taught that there is a spiritual presence of Christ, unattached to the bread and wine, in the Eucharist. Through the action of the Holy Spirit, Calvin argued, this presence lifts the faithful "up on the wings of faith to heaven," where they spiritually commune with Christ. Calvin also

The Eucharist

rejected the idea of the Eucharist as a sacrifice of expiation. He saw the sacrifice as the prayers, praise, and thanksgiving offered in the worship of God. Thus, there was no need, in his belief, for a priesthood to offer sacrifice. He, too, saw all Christians as priests in Christ, who had been ordained by God and consecrated according to the order of Melchizedek.

Zwingli rejected the concepts of the sacrifice of the Mass and a priesthood to offer the sacrifice. He considered the bread and wine that was eaten sacramentally as symbolic of Christ. According to Zwingli, the elements remained bread and wine but served as a reminder of Christ. The Lord's Supper, therefore, was a memorial service that reminded the participants of the Last Supper, the Passion, and the death of Jesus. It let them express their faith in the redemption he brought to the world and, at the same time, reminded them of their duty to follow his commands.

David Powers in *The Sacrifice We Offer* summarizes the five main problems the Reformers had with Catholic teachings and practices related to the Eucharist. First, the Reformers disapproved of what they saw as the automatic application of grace without faith or devotion on the part of the one who received it. They also rejected the idea that the Eucharist could benefit those who did not communicate at the Mass or who were absent or dead. In addition, the reformers would not accept the importance of the celebrating priest apart from the community. They objected, as well, to the idea of the Mass being a propitiatory sacrifice rather than one of thanksgiving, since this implied human mediation between God and a sinner. Finally, they protested against the practice of honoring saints at Masses, seeing this veneration as a substitute for the satisfaction worked by Christ.

Interpretations: Trent and Beyond

There is no denying that abuses in eucharistic practices had caused some loss of the New Testament sense of a ritual meal done "in memory of me." Whether the abuses were as widespread and destructive as the Reformers maintain is still subject to debate. Certainly, there were problems with the abuses and with some of the late medieval theology that contributed to their growth and continuation. Yet not all eucharistic theology gave credence to the abusive practices.

As Powers points out, some historians, looking at the cultural setting of the late Middle Ages, find that the eucharistic practices actually met the religious and social needs of the community. Other historians think that the positive theology of the twelfth and thirteenth centuries was betrayed by the practices of the next two centuries. Thus, the Catholic apologists who responded to the Reformers, along with the formulators of the decrees of the Council of Trent, felt justified in defending many practices and much of the theory of the Eucharist from the earlier medieval period.

The Council of Trent (1545-1563), the longest ecumenical council, formulated the Church's response to the challenges of the Reformation. It published three statements

The Eucharist

directly related to the Eucharist. At its thirteenth session in October of 1551 it announced the *Decree on the Most Holy Eucharist.* At session twenty-one in July of 1562 *The Doctrine on Communion under both Species and That of Little Children* was passed. Finally in September of 1562 at session twenty-two, it published *The Doctrine on the Most Holy Sacrifice of the Mass.*

The decree on the Eucharist originally had focused on refuting the errors of the reformers. The articles of the decree were debated intermittently from February of 1548 through July of 1562. In its final form, the document affirmed that Christ was truly, really, and substantially contained under the appearance of bread and wine. Though not a physical presence, it was a real—and not just a spiritual—presence. The document also stated that the action by which the whole substance of bread and wine is changed into the body and blood of Christ is "appropriately and rightly called transubstantiation by the Catholic Church." Thus, the Council gave official Church approval to this theory.

At the same time, the decree forbade the teaching, preaching, and believing of anything that differed from its teaching on the Eucharist. Moreover, it condemned as heretical the Reformers' beliefs about the Eucharist.

In the decree on both species and on the reception of communion by children, the Council Fathers rejected the criticism of the reformers on these two matters. The Council taught that Christ is in every particle of bread and every drop of wine, making it unnecessary for the laity to receive both species. They also held that children, by virtue of

Mary G. Durkin

their rebirth in baptism, do not need the spiritual benefit of the sacrament until they can sin deliberately. Earlier, the Church had practiced communion under both species with young children participating, but the decree defended this change on the basis of the authority God gave to the apostles' successors to regulate church practices.

The decree on the Mass was debated originally in December of 1551 and again in January of 1552 but was dropped with the adjournment of the Council in April of that year. It was not considered again until January of 1562. In its final form, it decreed that the Mass was instituted by Christ—but as a sacrifice, not as a sacrament. Although a sacrifice, the Mass, according to the decree, did not detract from Christ's sacrifice on the cross because the Mass was an unbloody sacrifice. As Christ's offering of himself, it was as satisfying to God as the offering of the cross and was not affected adversely by the character of the priest celebrating the Mass. Likewise, to be valid, it did not depend on the participation of the people attending the Mass nor did it require them to receive communion. Communion was viewed as the reception of the sacrament, the host, rather than as a part of the sacramental action.

The contemporary Catholic studying these conciliar decrees must bear in mind that the pronouncements were formulated over a period of many years. Even when they were promulgated, all bishops were not in complete agreement. Powers concludes that the majority of theologians and bishops did not agree that the Mass was an offering of the body and blood of Christ over and above his sacrifice on the cross. He also notes that while the Council approved of

The Eucharist

offering Masses for the living and the dead, it did not, even after much debate, offer a theoretical explanation for this practice.

Powers also points out that the Council of Trent did not explain how thanksgiving and propitiation, both related to the nature of sacrifice, are related to one another in the Mass. Furthermore, the Council did not propose a theology of redemption which could help explain how the Mass related to the Last Supper, the resurrection and Christ's heavenly intercession. Council members were limited to explaining how the Mass related to the cross, the main focus on the prevailing theology of redemption.

Powers notes, however, that the Council was primarily concerned with the role of the priest offering the Mass. No matter which topics of eucharistic theology or practice were addressed, Council members were always conscious of the sacramental activity of the priest. As a result of this focus, the laity after the Council remained passive observers of the actions of the priest as he offered the sacrifice for them. This hierarchical perspective continued to make sense to the bishops even though the Reformers criticized its infringement on the individual's relationship with God.

Church historians agree that the Council of Trent, while giving official approval to the theology and many of the practices of the Middle Ages, also solidified eucharistic practices and theology in a way the Church had been unable to do previously. As Joseph Martos summarizes in *Doors to the Sacred,* "(the Council) was both the capstone of eight centuries of liturgical development and the foun-

Mary G. Durkin

dation stone of four centuries of liturgical stability." Some observers would add that a stability of that length eventually leads to stagnation.

In addition, by directing the Pope to eliminate the abuses of the liturgy, the Council also gave him authority over it. The Council members thus gave up their own independence in liturgical matters. To eliminate eucharistic abuses, Pope St. Pius V in 1570 promulgated the Tridentine Missal. It was similar to the first missal, printed in 1474, and fashioned after a Mass book from the early thirteenth century. The difference was external—no one could deviate from the directives in the Tridentine Missal without explicit approval from Rome. In 1588, Pope Sixtus V set up the Congregation of Rites to oversee adherence to the directives. Until the 1960s, there was little deviation from this missal.

After reviewing this history of eucharistic practices and eucharistic interpretations prior to Vatican II, a contemporary Catholic can begin to understand how the Eucharist, originally a sacramental action using sacramental objects, came to be looked upon as a sacramental object. From this historical perspective, post-Vatican II attempts to emphasize the sacramental action of the Eucharist do not threaten the basic beliefs of the Catholic community.

PART THREE

THE EUCHARIST IN THE MODERN WORLD

CHAPTER FIVE

From Silent Mass to Eucharistic Celebration

ONE obvious sign of the changes in the Catholic Church since the Second Vatican Council is the way in which Catholics now celebrate the Eucharist. Although still popularly referred to as the "Mass," this celebration is different—both in practice and interpretation—from the "Mass" of the previous five hundred or more years. While Vatican II provided the ecclesial impetus for changes in the Mass, the theological underpinnings for such changes began to emerge in the nineteenth century. Once again, contemporary Catholics who want a deeper appreciation of the Eucharist need to consider why the Council, eager to make the Church responsive to the modern world, initiated changes in the Mass.

Most Catholics attending a Mass in the late 1950s had no idea how this Mass had evolved from the ritual meal of the New Testament accounts. Indeed, they probably did not

Mary G. Durkin

even know that the Eucharist had begun as a ritual meal. The Mass they attended in the 1950s was practically a carbon copy of the Tridentine Mass of 1570, which had been the norm for as long as anyone could remember.

It is not surprising, therefore, that Catholics in the first half of the twentieth century believed that the Mass followed a ritual established by Christ or his earliest followers. For at least 400 years, a similar Mass had been the standard worship of Catholics. For over 1,000 years, most Catholics had not understood the language in which the Mass was said. Long before the 1950s, passive attendance at a mysterious event was an accepted way of worship in the Catholic community.

At least the missals used by Catholic laity in the 1950s let them follow the ceremony carried out, silently for the most part, by the priest in the sanctuary. The Latin prayers the priest prayed were on one page, and the vernacular translation was on the page facing it. Prior to the late 1800s, the laity did not have access to a guide to the Mass. In the 1880s, the first Latin missals were published. Then, in the late 1890s, the Church lifted its prohibition against translating the Roman missal, finally making possible minimal participation by the laity in the "Sacrifice of the Mass."

While this Sacrifice of the Mass seems a far cry from the ritual meal of the New Testament, the Mass still played a sacramental role in the life of the Church and in the lives of the lay members of the community. The meaning of a religious symbol is that which the community imparts to it. What people did at the Tridentine Mass and what it meant to them was different from what the early followers of

The Eucharist

Jesus did and what it meant. Still, the Mass captured the sense of mystery people experienced in the world of the late Middle Ages and the several centuries that followed. While the Church did not consider the Mass a sacramental action, the ritual did contribute to a sense of God's presence in the midst of the community that gathered when it was offered.

In the 1950s, the Roman Mass, as the Tridentine Mass was then called, continued to separate eucharistic piety from what originally had been a eucharistic celebration. It also indirectly encouraged the laity to engage in non-eucharistic practices during the celebration of the Mass. Eucharistic piety included reception of communion before Mass, spiritual communion, infrequent reception of communion, adoration of the host, forty-hours devotion, benediction, and elaborate First Communion festivities. Conducting novena services while the Mass was being said silently at the altar, using devotional prayer books, and praying the rosary privately or publicly during Mass are but three examples of non-eucharistic practices.

The sacred elements, particularly the host, continued to be sacramental objects. The host's sacredness, however, had little connection with the Sacrifice of the Mass, save for the moment of elevation and, for some, the reception of communion.

Under the continuing influence of Jansenism, which contended that Holy Communion was the reward of merit rather than the food of salvation, the concept of the laity's unworthiness persisted. Jansenistic practices discouraged reception of communion. For example, a confessor was

Mary G. Durkin

given the power to determine not only whether a person was free from both mortal and venial sin but whether the person desired to avoid future inclinations to sin. On the basis of his evaluation, the confessor could regulate the number of times a week a repentant sinner could receive communion. In some cases, he would assign a penance that prohibited the person from receiving communion for a specific length of time.

Eucharistic theology after Trent did little to encourage the reuniting of sacramental objects with sacramental action. The Council's emphasis on the Real Presence, communion, and the Sacrifice of the Mass set the tone for most Catholic theology through the 1950s. There was little innovative theology throughout that long period. Theologians primarily addressed questions of how the Mass was a sacrifice or how the Real Presence in the sacred elements could be analyzed in more detail. They separated the theology of the Sacrifice of the Mass from the theology of the sacrament of the Eucharist. Catholics, both clerical and lay, saw this separation as the normative Catholic view. Even in the 1980s, as one contemporary writer wryly observes, there are some priests, trained in that tradition, who consider the Mass only a sacrifice and not a sacrament. There also are a considerable number of lay people, raised in the same tradition, who think the same way.

The Beginnings of a Restoration

Nevertheless, during the nineteenth century, movements developed in both theology and liturgy which caused Cath-

The Eucharist

olic thinkers to reassess the continuing, slavish application of earlier eucharistic practices and interpretations. Nineteenth-century and then twentieth-century theologians and liturgists began to question if the Mass and the Eucharist had always been celebrated as they were in the 1600s and 1700s. Contemporary efforts to restore the union of sacrifice and sacrament in a ritual action modeled more faithfully on the original eucharistic celebration owe their impetus to these movements. Several papal documents of the twentieth century also contributed to new directions in eucharistic thought.

The Benedictine revival of earlier forms of liturgical practices began with Dom Prosper Guéranger's studies of the liturgical year. His work grew out of the nineteenth century's renewed interest in the Middle Ages. As libraries uncovered ancient documents and as more rigid historical investigation emerged, Guéranger discovered people in earlier times had participated in the liturgy. He also learned that there had existed varying interpretations of the Eucharist and not just the one presented by Trent.

Although by today's standards Guéranger's work seems too academic, he stimulated a revival of Benedictine interest in the liturgy. The Benedictines had refounded their abbey at Solesmes in France in 1832. Guéranger was part of this community, and inspired by his discoveries, the monks there nurtured a monastic liturgy with Gregorian chant. They spread their new liturgical ideas through the word of those who came for retreats and study and through their publication, *L'Année Liturgique*. The Benedictines also were the first to encourage people to use missals and to

Mary G. Durkin

pray along with the priest at Mass.

The liturgical movement had its quasi-official beginning at a conference in Malines, Belgium, in 1909, with leadership provided by Dom Lambert Beauduin of Mount César in Louvain. Participants at the conference asked for a vernacular translation of the Roman missal, a centering of Christian life on the liturgy, and a restoration of Gregorian Chant. They proposed retreats at various centers of liturgical worship. Seeing the liturgy as the fundamental means for instructing Catholics in life and faith, they concluded that the active participation of the faithful in the liturgy would nourish and deepen spiritual life.

Beauduin's work *La Piété de l'Eglise,* published in 1914, is considered by liturgists to provide the basis for the fundamental principles of the liturgical movement. He argued for a correct understanding of Incarnation, of the Church as the body of Christ, and of the sacrifice of Christ. He taught that the Incarnation demands an appreciation of the dignity of human life and of all creation. In addition, he proposed that the Church as the body of Christ should develop a deep sense of community in its worship and life. He believed, moreover, that the sacrifice of Christ encourages people to live out the eucharistic sacrifice by offering their own lives along with the offering of Christ.

The early liturgical movement was more pastoral than academic. Its aim was to recall all Catholics to active participation in the liturgy, which would be more than simply a restoration of past liturgical styles. The liturgists saw worship—especially the Eucharist—as the source of renewal in the Church.

The Eucharist

The Benedictine monks of St. John's Abbey in Collegeville, Minnesota, led the twentieth-century effort in the United States to encourage lay people to understand and participate in the Mass. Under the direction of Dom Virgil Michel, the Abbey was a major center of liturgical renewal by the late 1920s. During the 1920s, 1930s, and 1940s, it had liturgical music and prayers in English. Its publication, *Orate Fratres,* eventually renamed *Worship,* was, like the movement at the time, pastorally oriented. Articles were written for the laity and parish priests.

Pope St. Pius X's interest in eucharistic piety also helped to dispel the eucharistic excesses of Jansenism. In 1903, Pius X encouraged lay participation through the use of a chant. He also encouraged Catholics to receive communion on a more regular basis. In 1910, he discouraged the post-Trent practice of delaying First Communion until a child was twelve to sixteen years old. Instead, he set the age of seven as the time for this first reception.

During the period between the two world wars, the center of liturgical renewal moved to Germany, though it also continued to grow in Austria, France, and Belgium. A backlash developed against the movement, however, among those who felt it was a threat to the traditional teachings of the Church. As a result, the tasks of the movement during this period centered on articulating a sound theology of liturgy.

Initial work in this direction began at the Abbey of Maria Laach in the Rhineland. The Abbey became the center for the scientific study of the liturgy. Abbot Ildefons Herwegen and Dom Odo Casel pioneered developing an

Mary G. Durkin

apologetic for the movement. Their publication, *Ecclesia Orans,* began in 1918 and, through its large circulation, spread the message far beyond the Abbey.

This new attention to liturgy caused liturgical theology to be recognized as a legitimate field in theological studies. In addition to the monks of Maria Laach, the giants of this period who inspired liturgical studies were Josef Jungmann, Jean Danielou, and Louis Bouyer.

Other great European abbeys also encouraged lay people to work for liturgical reform. Dom Columba Marmion at Maredsous emphasized biblical and liturgical spirituality. The Abbey at Beuron strove to enhance liturgical art. Together with the theological interest generated by Maria Laach, these abbeys educated the laity while creating an experience of eucharistic worship which had long been absent in the Catholic community.

The studies of Jungmann and the Anglican Gregory Dix, as well as other liturgical research during the Second World War, uncovered most of the historical evidence discussed in the earlier chapters of this book. Their work gave liturgists the evidence they needed to prove that eucharistic practices had varied prior to Trent. Other scholarship from the period during the Second World War concluded that there had been interpretations of the Eucharist which had differed from those developed by the Scholastics. The research suggested a search for a new philosophical basis for liturgical reform and theological reflection on the Eucharist.

This research was not ignored by the *magisterium* (the teaching authorities of the Church). In 1947, Pope Pius

The Eucharist

XII published *Mediator Dei,* an encyclical on the liturgy. Some scholars consider it the most crucial liturgical document ever written by a Pope. It made an important contribution to the liturgical movement, giving it a status within the official Church.

Part Two of the encyclical addresses eucharistic issues, covering in four separate chapters the nature of Eucharistic Sacrifice, the role of the faithful in Eucharistic Sacrifice, Holy Communion, and Adoration of the Eucharist. The Pope confirmed the intrinsic connection of the Mass with Calvary, noting that the four ends of sacrifice are praise, thanksgiving, propitiation, and petition. He spoke of "the priesthood of the laity," and a laity who, through their baptism, share in the priesthood of Christ himself. He encouraged the frequent reception of communion, even suggesting that, when possible, people attending Mass should receive hosts consecrated at that particular Mass.

In a reflection on the Adoration of the Eucharist, Pius XII argued in favor of the practice since the Eucharist is both a Sacrifice and a Sacrament. As a sacrament, however, it differs from the other sacraments because it both causes grace and contains "the Author of grace himself." He believed the Church was enriched by the cult of the Eucharist. Through the various practices of the cult, he argued, the faithful testify to the faith of the Church, which sees Christ present in the Eucharist.

In the encyclical, the Pope tried to establish a middle ground between those who were pushing for a change in the eucharistic ritual and those who wanted to maintain the *status quo.* He therefore endorsed some important tradi-

Mary G. Durkin

tional attitudes, emphasizing, for example, that the laity were not priests in the same way as ordained ministers were. He also cautioned that liturgical piety is no substitute for personal piety. Finally, he argued that communion by the faithful is not necessary for the "completion of the sacrifice" of the Mass.

In 1951, the Pope took a first step toward recovering ancient eucharistic practices by restoring the evening celebration of the Paschal Vigil, the Church's oldest liturgical ritual other than the original meals of the New Testament. Until the seventh century, this vigil, which celebrated the Passion, death, and resurrection of Jesus, was held on the Saturday night and Sunday morning of Easter. In the Middle Ages, the celebration began earlier and earlier in the day. The Roman missal of 1570 finally ordered that the service could not be celebrated after mid-day on Saturday, even though the liturgy continued to sing of the holy "night" when Christ freed humans from sin. The 1951 restoration was experimental and contained partly revised texts and rites. Then, in 1955, the entire Holy Week liturgy was revised. That same year, Pius XII issued *De musica sacre,* which contained guidelines for lay participation in the liturgy.

Other modest liturgical reforms approved by the Church in the 1950s included allowing an evening Mass on Sundays and holy days in some dioceses and shortening the compulsory fast before communion from midnight the night before to three hours before receiving communion. These reforms were designed to meet the needs of people in urban settings who were unable to attend morning Mass and

The Eucharist

whose working patterns made prolonged pre-Communion fasting difficult—if not impossible. Other pastoral needs eventually called for even greater reform.

In the late 1950s, most Catholics, lay and clerical, were unaware of the ferment caused by the liturgical movement. As a result, they attributed the changes in the Mass following Vatican II to the Council itself. Many scholars, however, recognized that the liturgical movement, with its thought-provoking discoveries and its calls for reform, served as a major impetus to the calling of the Council.

Vatican II and the Eucharist

Reforming and renewing the liturgy to make it responsive to the contemporary world was, from the beginning, an important item on the agenda of the bishops gathered for the Council. While the world media waited for pronouncements on major problems facing the Church in the modern world, the bishops debated issues on the liturgy. A preparatory commission was established in 1960 with Jungmann and Johannes Quasten, a renowned expert in the Patristic era, among its scholarly members. The consulters to the commission were also known for their liturgical studies. Of the twenty-five experts then chosen to advise the commission of Council members charged with drafting a constitution, twelve were members of this preparatory commission. The insights of recent liturgical scholarship were evident in the Council's theological and liturgical treatment of the Eucharist.

Mary G. Durkin

Between October 22 and November 13, 1962, the proposed constitution on the liturgy was debated at fifteen sessions before its text was approved—in principle. Discussions of the text continued, however, and amendments were introduced. Finally, at the 1963 session, an overwhelming majority of Council members approved the *Constitution on the Sacred Liturgy*. Pope Paul VI promulgated it on December 4, 1963. Thus, liturgical reform was the impetus not only for the Council but also for the first constitution that was to emerge from the Council.

Chapter Two of the Constitution presents the Council's teaching on the Mass. It first states what Christ did: the Savior "instituted the Eucharistic sacrifice of his Body and Blood" at the Last Supper on the night he was betrayed. Then, it interprets the meaning of that action: he did it to continue the sacrifice of the cross until he comes again, thereby giving the Church "a memorial of his death and resurrection, a sacrament of love, a sign of unity, a bond of charity, a paschal banquet." In this banquet, the bishops wrote, "Christ is consumed, the mind is filled with grace, and a pledge of future glory is given to us."

In one passage on the Eucharist, the Constitution describes how it moves people to covenant. From all liturgy but particularly from the Eucharist, "grace is poured forth upon us as from a fountain, and the sanctification of men in Christ and the glorification of God to which all other activities are directed" are achieved.

The document also gives directives on practical matters of eucharistic liturgy. It addresses specific issues, including the revision of the ritual of the Mass, the use of the Bible,

The Eucharist

the homily, the prayer of the faithful, the vernacular in liturgy, communion under both species, and concelebration. Moreover, the Constitution calls for the participation of the laity, directing them to offer Christ not only through the priest but also with him. The bishops expressed the hope that, in this way, the laity would learn to offer themselves as well. All these directives for eucharistic ritual were designed to make participation possible.

In the late 1980s, the theology underlying this Constitution might be considered less than progressive. Yet on a practical level, the Constitution called for more changes in the Eucharist than had been made in the previous four centuries. Later conciliar documents went on to address eucharistic issues both directly and indirectly.

The *Constitution on the Church,* for example, proclaims that whenever the sacrifice of the cross is celebrated, the work of redemption is carried out. It addresses the role of the faithful and the role of the priest in celebrating this expression and this cause of unity for believers.

According to the *Constitution on the Church,* the "People of God" take part in the eucharistic sacrifice, which is the source and summit of Christian life. In this sacrifice, the faithful offer Christ to God and offer themselves along with him. Strengthened by the body of Christ in Communion, they concretely manifest their unity as the People of God. This is the unity the sacrament both signifies and realizes. The priest exercises his priestly function most fully when, in the eucharistic gathering, he acts in the person of Christ and proclaims Christ's mystery. By these actions, he unites the offering of the faithful to the sacrifice of Christ, making present the unique sacrifice of Christ.

The *Decree on the Eastern Churches* recognizes the love the separated Eastern churches have for the sacred liturgy, which contributes to the building up of the Church of God. The *Decree on Ecumenism* asserts the Church's belief that the absence of Holy Orders in the separated churches fails to preserve fully the eucharistic mystery. The document acknowledges, however, that when the separated churches celebrate the Lord's Supper, they, too, signify "life in communion with Christ and await his coming in glory." Thus, it argues that the doctrines of the Lord's Supper, the other sacraments, worship, and ministry in the Church should be subjects for dialogue between the churches.

The practical matters of implementing ritual reforms made it obvious to Catholics in the 1960s that the Church was embarking on a course of drastic change. This shift was particularly startling to those Catholics, lay and clerical, who were unfamiliar with the liturgical, historical, and theological research that led up to the Council. Some modern commentators on the Council have concluded that most of the bishops were not conscious of the impact changes in the eucharistic liturgy would have on the very people they hoped would "manifest the unity of the People of God."

That changes in eucharistic celebrations should signal a change in Catholic self-understanding is not surprising. The Eucharist is the core sacrament of the Catholic sacramental system, and the system is an expression of religious meaning for Catholics. Therefore, changes in the way

The Eucharist

people celebrate the Eucharist can change how they view the Eucharist. Their new perception of the Eucharist can produce a religious understanding attuned to their new experience of it.

Unfortunately, the implementation of Council reforms often has been accompanied by a sense of confusion on the part of both clergy and laity. Although most people have responded favorably to the liturgical changes, they often are not sure what the "new" liturgy is supposed to accomplish. In many instances, those responsible for implementing change did what Church authorities told them to do without asking for explanations. Consequently, the only explanations they could offer their congregations were that the bishop, pope, or Council had ordered the changes.

A contemporary Catholic aware of the ferment created by the Council must remember that the eucharistic theology and liturgical practices suggested by the Council were themselves the end products of over a century of pastoral and scholarly insights. The Council made these insights available to a much wider audience. Opening windows increased the possibility that Catholics would call for further development of a eucharistic theology and a eucharistic ritual that would take into account the experiences of the people to whom they were addressed. For the Church in the modern world, eucharistic practices must relate what people do as a result of their understanding of Jesus' command to do this "in memory of me."

CHAPTER SIX

Post-Vatican II

THE confusion that accompanied making a Church that maintained a fortress mentality for over 400 years suddenly responsive to the needs of the modern world is understandable. When an institution appears to change, the members are apt to be uneasy especially if, in their eyes, the institution had the definitive and unchanging answers to their religious questions. When the foundational ritual of that institution, also thought to be immutable, undergoes radical change, the members know that the change is more than simply a theoretical discussion, unrelated to their lives. They realize they are being asked to adjust their understanding of how their faith and their lives interrelate. Furthermore, they sense that their certitude about the answers to some questions of faith might not be as absolute as they thought it to be.

Many Catholics, both religious leaders and general members, welcomed this change, however. They had experienced the rigidity of the Counter-Reformation mentality as stifling. Other leaders and church members, however, were not pleased with what they saw as an undermining of the truth of their faith. Both groups saw the changes

The Eucharist

in the Eucharist as weekly or even daily reinforcing their response to the post-Vatican II Church.

A contemporary Catholic hoping to understand the Eucharist in the midst of the conflicting messages since the Council, must begin by reviewing the eucharistic interpretations and practices since the Council. Every Catholic has been affected by the Council's attempt to renew the Eucharist. The *magisterium* implemented Eucharist practices suggested by the Council and also condemned Eucharist abuses. Theologians and liturgists moved well beyond their pre-conciliar reflections and opened up new areas of debate. Lay Catholics now find themselves expected to participate in the Eucharist rather than be passive observers. Priests as presiders must be conscious of the important role of the other participants if the eucharistic celebration is to be an effective symbol of Christ's presence in the midst of the community.

The Magisterium and Eucharistic Practices

When the Council Fathers decreed that the Order of the Mass should be modified, they wanted to return it "to the vigor" it had in the days of the Patristic Fathers. In January, 1964, Pope Paul VI set up a commission to begin the process of implementing the *Constitution on the Sacred Liturgy*. He ordered educational centers to teach the instruction on the liturgy outlined by the Council. He also called for the establishment of diocesan commissions to promote an understanding of the liturgy.

Mary G. Durkin

Recognizing that it would take time and research to make the revisions called for by the Council, the commission instituted interim steps before announcing a final revision of the Mass ritual. Initially, parts of the Mass were translated into the vernacular. In Advent of 1964 the congregation began reciting the Gloria, the Creed, the responses, and the chants. At the same time, the prayers of the faithful were added, and the Last Gospel was eliminated. The prayer at the end of the Offertory known as the "Secret" was renamed the "Prayer over the Gifts" and said aloud. The Canon was said aloud with the people saying "Amen" after the doxology.

This was followed by a translation of the entire Mass. Finally, in April, 1969, the Apostolic Constitution, *Missale Romanum* was issued instituting the New Order of the Mass. Its use was not to be compulsory for two years.

The purpose of this Order of the Mass was to simplify the rites. However, care was "taken to preserve their substance." As a result, those extraneous features that were added over time or were duplicated were eliminated, especially those having to do with "the preparation of the bread and wine, the Breaking of the Bread, and the Communion." The Constitution was accompanied by the *Institutio Generalis,* a justification of the changes and an explanation of different parts of the Mass.

In this final Order of the Mass, most of the changes from the interim Mass remain. Now, however, there is a penitential rite at the beginning of Mass, and the Liturgy of the Word is a critical part of the ritual. The addition of a responsorial psalm and an Old Testament reading on

The Eucharist

Sundays and holy days, along with the choice of biblical texts from the various readings allotted for these days, emphasizes the importance of the Bible in this celebration of the faith community.

The Offertory underwent many changes. The commission found that the prayers previously said by the priest in a low voice were repetitious and intruded on the Eucharistic Prayer. So, they eliminated those prayers said over bread and wine, the psalm at the washing of the hands, and the oblation prayer to the Holy Trinity. Thus, after 1,100 years, the gifts are no longer offered to the Trinity. The offertory prayers are shorter and modelled on the prayer of the Jewish father at a ritual meal.

Three eucharist Prayers were added, as well as eighty new Prefaces. The Canon was altered slightly. Now, the words "which will be given up for you" are said after "This is my Body." "Do this in memory of me" replaces "Whenever you do this." The proclamation of the mystery of faith is made after the consecration.

The prayers after the Our Father have been simplified with the prayer for peace now said before the Lamb of God. The congregation is invited to share a sign of peace. The consecrated bread is broken at the Lamb of God. A silent time of thanksgiving comes after communion, and the prayers of ablution may be omitted.

Thus, the *magisterium* gave its endorsement to a radical departure from the way in which Catholics had worshiped prior to the Council. Needless to say, in the transition period following the initial changes, many questions have arisen about implementing them correctly. There also has

Mary G. Durkin

been some resistance to change. In addition, the freedom to change encouraged a spirit of experimentation which had not been present when the Tridentine Mass was in use.

The *magisterium* responded to questions and confusion over the liturgy with many official statements. In the period up to 1975 alone, 120 documents dealing with the liturgy were issued. These directives covered a variety of issues: stipends, the eucharistic fast, communion outside of Mass, communion under both species, communion in the hand, extraordinary ministers, communion more than once a day, concelebration, communion in hospitals, First Communion, Mass for special groups, reservation of the Blessed Sacrament, liturgical music, the homily, women serving the priest, the obligation to use the Roman Missal, and eucharist prayers for children's Masses.

The official Church also issued directives regarding what it considered to be abuses in the liturgy following the changes suggested by the Council. In September, 1965, Paul VI issued an encyclical letter, *Mysterium Fidei,* to counteract the rush toward eucharistic anarchy Rome saw in some practices and theories. Among those he cited were: an exaggerated emphasis on communal Mass over private Mass, distorted ideas about sacramental sign and symbol, disregard for Trent's statement on transubstantiation, and the idea that Christ is no longer present in the hosts after the Mass is over.

The Pope referred to the Eucharist as a mystery of faith found in the sacrifice of the Mass. He also supported the sacramental presence of Christ, the theory of transubstantiation, and the cult of the Eucharist. Other decrees from

The Eucharist

Rome dealt with the obligation to use the New Order of Mass found in the Roman Missal and censured the use of experimental eucharistic prayers.

Pope John Paul II in *Inaestimabile Donum* in April 1980, summed up many of Rome's worries regarding the abuses of the post-conciliar era. The document is considered an indictment against errors as well as a program for reform. The Pope expressed concern about the confusion of the roles of priest and laity seen in the shared recitation of the Eucharistic Prayer and in lay people distributing communion when the priest did not. He also saw a loss of the sense of the sacred with the abandoning of vestments and with the unnecessary celebration of Mass outside a church. In addition, he found a disregard for the ecclesial character of the liturgy in the use of private texts and unapproved eucharistic prayers and in the manipulation of texts for social and political ends. He forbade anyone to add, remove, or change anything in the liturgy on their own authority.

John Paul II also has addressed the issue of the Eucharist and divorced and remarried Catholics. In *Familiaris Consortio* in 1981, he reaffirmed the practice of not allowing divorced and remarried persons to receive communion for two reasons. First of all, he wrote, their state and condition of life objectively contradict the sign of love between Christ and the Church effected by the sacrament. In addition, the faithful would be confused regarding the Church's teaching about the indissolubility of marriage. He reiterated this teaching in *Reconciliatio et Paenitentia* in 1984, saying the divorced and remarried could avail themselves of communion and penance only after obtaining the required dispensations (i.e., an annulment).

The 1983 Code of Canon Law gives rules for the Eucharist regarding the minister, participation rites, ceremonies, intercommunion, the time and place for the celebration, the reservation and veneration of the Eucharist, and stipends. In 1980, Ladislas Orsy developed guidelines that help in interpreting and applying these laws. In summarizing Orsy's system, John Huels contends that an interpreter must view liturgical law as a system with a historical and theological context that must be understood in the light of the pastoral aim of all liturgical law.

Huels suggests that interpreters of liturgical law should have a sound liturgical education. However, since implementers of the law at the local level cannot be expected to be grounded in the same way, those who fashion the laws must be faithful to history and good theology, be familiar with local cultures and customs and make provisions for diversity and adaptation. If that is the case, the laws will allow for eucharistic celebrations that bring together the experiences of congregations and the experience of Christ, who is remembered in the celebration.

The Magisterium and Ecumenical Discussions of the Eucharist

Catholic ecumenical discussions following the Council have covered many areas of church life and thought. Social action, theological interchanges, and some shared worship

The Eucharist

services have all contributed to a desire to work toward unity with other Christian churches. The *magisterium* has been involved in these discussions either by appointing members to commissions established for dialogue or by its response to reports of these commissions. Given the importance of the Eucharist for the identity and life of a Christian church, past differences in eucharistic interpretation and practice have been a primary topic for dialogue.

Eucharistic conversations with Anglicans have been under the auspice of the Anglican-Roman Catholic International Commission formed as a result of an agreement between Paul VI and the Archbishop of Canterbury, Michael Ramsey, in 1966. The commission held its first meeting in 1970 and, in the fall of 1971, issued a report stating they had reached substantial agreement on the Eucharist. The report dealt with the issues of the mystery of the Eucharist, the Eucharist and the sacrifice of Christ, and the presence of Christ. Optimistically, the members felt that this agreement meant there was no longer any obstacle to unity from the point of view of eucharistic doctrine.

The statement met with much criticism, however, leading to a follow-up 1979 *Elucidation* of the earlier report. The second report explains its use of the terms *anamnesis* and sacrifice (memorial) in its discussion of the Eucharist.

The Sacred Congregation for the Doctrine of the Faith issued the Church's response to the work of the commission in a report sent to Pope John Paul II in 1982. While praising the notable effort toward reconciliation carried out by the commission, it also noted negative features of

Mary G. Durkin

the report. In particular, the Church's response found fault with the claim of substantial agreement and with a certain ambiguity in some statements. In addition, the Congregation found doctrinal difficulties in the treatment of the Eucharist as sacrifice and of the Real Presence. In both instances, the Congregation faults the joint commission for an inadequate interpretation of the teachings of the Council of Trent.

Lutheran-Roman Catholic discussions on the Eucharist have been carried out by the Lutheran-Roman Catholic Joint Commission which published a report, *The Eucharist,* in 1980. The commission members unanimously passed the document stating they had reached agreement on significant points and expressed confidence that the remaining issues will be "clarified mutually." The tasks for the future still include overcoming disagreement on controversial positions and working out an agreeable liturgical form.

A third important ecumenical conversation on the Eucharist is that carried out under the auspices of the Faith and Order Commission of the World Council of Churches. Although the Catholic Church is not a member of the World Council of Churches, it does belong to the Faith and Order Commission. At the January 1982, meeting of the commission in Lima, over one hundred theologians (including Catholic theologians) adopted the *Baptism, Eucharist, and Ministry* statement of the commission. They agreed to send it to the over three hundred member churches for their "reception" (a term which lacks common agreement among the churches).

The Eucharist

Alan Falconer describes the theology of the report as rich and challenging to the eucharistic theology of all the churches, and yet one, he feels, all the traditions could accept. The statement places the institution of the Eucharist in the context of the Old Testament meals that affirm the Covenant, thus making the Eucharist the New Covenant. The Eucharist is seen as a community meal of thanksgiving (*berakah*) and memory (*anamnesis*). Christ is present to the community through this *anamnesis*. The report emphasizes the once-and-for-all nature of the sacrifice of Christ yet acknowledges that the authors of the report cannot say at what particular moment this presence takes place or in what manner. Yet they are in agreement that his presence is actualized through the Holy Spirit.

In these and other ecumenical discussions, participants, including some Catholics, believe that intercommunion, the sharing of one another's Eucharist, would help break down some of the obstacles still separating the churches. However, the Catholic position on intercommunion, as outlined in the 1983 Code of Canon Law, continues to oppose sharing of communion except with Orthodox churches. Protestants may receive communion in the Catholic Church only when there is a grave necessity and only with the permission of competent Church authority. Catholics may only receive communion in Churches that have a validly ordained priest, that is, one ordained by a bishop considered by the Church to be in apostolic succession. For Catholics this requirement of valid orders effectively rules out communion in all but the Orthodox churches.

Mary G. Durkin
The Magisterium and the Role of the Priest in the Eucharist

The Catholic understanding of priesthood and the link between priest and Eucharist are two issues the *magisterium* has had to address repeatedly during the upheaval following the Council. One unanticipated side effect of the environment of change engendered by the Council was the large exodus of men from the priesthood. Some left to marry. Others left out of a general sense of dissatisfaction. Of the latter, some felt the Church was changing too rapidly; others felt the pace of change was too slow.

Another side effect, also unexpected, is the question of the ordination of women. The bishops at the Council, like most other people in the late fifties and early sixties, had no idea of the revolution in women's role that was about to erupt in varying degrees throughout the world. Even if they had been aware of it, however, they probably never would have anticipated any serious challenge to the Church's all male clergy.

The Council's statements on priesthood acknowledge that priests are "marked with a special character and are so configured to Christ the Priest that they can act in the person of Christ the Head." The Council declared that priests exercise the office of Christ most fully when they act in the person of Christ in the eucharistic liturgy. Nevertheless, the Council's theology of priesthood often seems rooted in the episcopacy. In the Council's view, the priest, when connected with the bishop, shares in the authority of Christ.

The Eucharist

The New Code of Canon Law calls priests "helpers" and "advisers" of bishops. Responding to the crisis of priest defections, Paul VI in 1969 sent priests a special message, hoping to fortify their commitment and thereby contribute to an enrichment of the Eucharist. Under his leadership, the episcopal synod of 1971 had the priesthood as its theme.

Pope John Paul II is more explicit in his attention to the problems of the priesthood. He links the priestly office with the Eucharist saying, "A priest is worth what his Eucharistic life is worth." He has written numerous Holy Thursday letters for priests, seeing Holy Thursday as the feast of the priesthood and the Eucharist. He sees the Eucharist as the "principal and central *raison d'etre* of the priesthood." The Eucharist and the priesthood came into being at the institution of the Eucharist. He considers priests to be priests of Christ's priesthood and of his sacrifice in addition to being "priests for men."

From these various post-conciliar statements, it is obvious that the *magisterium* considers the theology of the priesthood to be intrinsically linked to the theology of the Eucharist. For them, there is no valid Eucharist without a valid priesthood. The priesthood is valid when it is linked to Christ's institution of the priesthood at the Last Supper. This interpretation is declared to be the correct understanding of the Catholic Tradition of the priesthood and of the Eucharist.

Tradition also is used as the basis for the *magisterium's* decisions about women's role in the liturgy. In instructions

Mary G. Durkin

regarding the Order of the Mass in 1969 and 1970, conferences of bishops were given permission to allow women to do the readings before the Gospel, providing there was no man capable of performing the reader's role. The women were to stand outside the sanctuary, however. In 1975, there was a minor alteration to the instruction, allowing conferences of bishops to designate a suitable place for the women to read.

The *magisterium* also excludes women from the role of altar server on the basis of tradition. In September 1970, in *Liturgicae Instaurationes,* the Congregation for Divine Worship maintained that the norms of Church tradition bar women from serving priests at the altar. They may, according to this document, do readings, announce the general intercessions, lead choirs, play musical instruments, read commentaries, and perform other roles "customarily filled by women in other settings." These roles might be ushering, organizing processions or taking up collections. Obviously, the *magisterium* did not see women as possible priests.

In October 1976, the Church responded to the request for ordination of women with *Inter Insigniores,* a Declaration on the Admission of Women to the Ministerial Priesthood. The Declaration maintains that the Church "has never felt that priestly or episcopal ordination can be validly conferred on women." This position is defended with references to Scripture and Church history, in which the framers of the statement can find no evidence of women celebrating the Eucharist.

Those who support the ordination of women point to re-

The Eucharist

cent biblical scholarship by both men and women which indicates that women did function in priestly roles, more than likely even presiding at the Eucharists they hosted in their homes. In addition, supporters of women's ordination consider it unjust that more than half the membership of the Church should be excluded from the leadership role of the priest both in the Eucharist and in Church life.

Pope John Paul II repeated the arguments of *Inter Insigniores* when he visited the United States in 1979. In addition, he declared that this was not an issue of human rights but the conviction of the Church about the particular dimension of the priesthood which God has chosen. The Church leadership believes that the call to men is in accord with the prophetic tradition.

During this period, the teaching authority of the Church continued to emphasize the importance of the key themes of earlier periods of Church history. Transubstantiation, the Real Presence, the Sacrifice of the Mass, and the Eucharist as a source of unity are mentioned repeatedly. In the period of transition, however, the *magisterium* obviously considered it important to exercise authority over liturgical practices as well.

Eucharist Theology after Vatican II

Discussion of the meaning of the Eucharist is not limited to the *magisterium*. Throughout the history of the Church, theologians have reflected on the meaning of the ritual in which the absent one is made present. At certain times these theologians have been in agreement with Church

Mary G. Durkin

authorities. At other times, they have not. In many instances, these theological reflections on the Eucharist have eventually found their way into the official teachings of the Church.

A mark of eucharistic interpretation since the Council has been the joining together of the theology of the Eucharist and the theology of the liturgy. This unity comes from the understanding of the Eucharist as sacramental action rather than just sacramental object.

The historical and biblical research that helped form the liturgical movement and infused the Council serves as a basis for developing many of the traditional eucharistic concepts in ways that might not have been considered in the Middle Ages or at the Council of Trent. In addition, new philosophical approaches suggest new categories for explaining basic truths of the faith. So, too, the study of symbols and symbolism explored in the first chapter helps explain what the community means by the liturgical action of a eucharistic celebration.

In addition to those interpretations that emphasize the Eucharist as sacrifice, as Real Presence, and as cause of unity, theologians see the Eucharist as meal, memorial, thanksgiving, eschatological challenge, justification, and impetus to social action. All these categories have roots in both Scripture and Tradition. Contemporary theologians, aware of these roots, seek to develop the categories in ways that have meaning for people in the modern world yet do not lose the validity of earlier interpretations.

Thus, theological discussions of transubstantiation, transignification, and transfinalization all try, philosophi-

The Eucharist

cally, to explain how the bread and wine become the body and blood of Christ. Proponents of each theory refer to how their ideas relate to what the Scholastics and Trent meant by transubstantiation.

The category of the Real Presence today includes discussions of Christ's presence in the entire eucharistic celebration and in the community that celebrates. Christ is seen as present in the Word of God as well as in the sacred elements. He is also considered present in the community that then takes him forth from the celebration. Though the presence is different in each instance, it is considered no less real.

The unity of which the Eucharist is both cause and effect is now seen as challenging those who participate in the Eucharist to join with each other both in the eucharistic celebration and in caring for those in need outside the community. In this way, they are making Christ's presence felt in much the same way he made it felt during his ministry. The concept of Eucharist as meal emphasizes the importance of this sharing with one another.

Understanding the Eucharist as sacrifice as well as memorial links the Last Supper with Christ's death and resurrection. The Eucharist becomes the way the Christian participates in the death and resurrection of Christ. The Eucharist is seen as a corporate action in which the community unites with the past in the present and points toward the future.

Liturgy is the place where Christians remember. It is also the place where they offer thanksgiving for the gift of Christ's life, death, and resurrection. In addition, it is

Mary G. Durkin

where they experience the call to unity and service. All these activities are possible because Christ at the Last Supper gave himself to his followers and told them to remember him. He continues to be present—really, truly, and substantially (though mysteriously and symbolically to the community that understands this presence)—whenever people gather in his memory to follow his example.

An important characteristic of much contemporary theology of the Eucharist is its attempt to connect the tradition of the Eucharist with the experiences of contemporary humans. When the theology is addressing fundamental issues, it considers the "common human experience" found in scientific investigations of humanity. When the theology is pastoral, it seeks to relate the insights uncovered in discourse about fundamental issues to the actual experiences of specific groups. Liberation theology, for example, uses the experience of oppression as starting point for understanding the meaning of the Eucharist. The method of pastoral theology that was developed by John Shea also begins with listening to human experience.

The Order of the Mass in Practice in 1988

Most Catholics, however, are not familiar with the discussions of theologians. Also, what little they know about pronouncements of the *magisterium* comes from brief, and often inaccurate, summaries in the secular press. For the majority of Catholics, any new appreciation of the

The Eucharist

meaning of the Eucharist comes from their experience of the Mass.

During the pre-conciliar years, people attending Mass seldom noticed any difference from one Mass to another. They might have complained because some priests were slower than others and some Sunday sermons focused on money but, for the most part, every Mass was the same. The same cannot be said of the Mass at the end of the twentieth century. Three official eucharistic celebrations during the fall of 1988 show how the changes initiated by the Council have resulted in different interpretations of how to celebrate the Eucharist in a way that reflects its sacramental power.

Twenty people staying at a house of prayer in the Arizona desert gather in a small chapel. A huge picture window behind the altar turns the cacti and birds of the desert into a living stained-glass window. Mosaics on the walls of the chapel commemorate events in Christ's life, some of them from the perspective of the Indians of the Arizona desert. The congregation gathers in a semi-circle around the altar, where the presiding priest recites the official prayers in an inclusive manner. A woman from the congregation reads the first biblical passage thoughtfully. The congregation responds with song and spoken words. The priest's homily relates the message of the scripture readings to the prayer experience of the congregation, also reminding them of their responsibility to the world beyond the house of prayer. The handshake of peace affirms the support of the group to each member. Another woman partic-

Mary G. Durkin

ipant assists in the distribution of the consecrated bread and wine. At the conclusion, some members remain in the chapel for private prayer. Others congregate outside the chapel for a short time before returning to their various tasks. There is a lingering sense of renewal from the making present in the desert of the absent one who is at the center of what life is all about.

Next, it is the Saturday evening Mass in a resort center in the West of Ireland. On the outside, the dark stone church appears foreboding. On the inside, the light does little to change that feeling. The lads (every male over twelve who is able to stand for the hour of the Mass) are gathered in the vestibule of the church. The females and males under the age of twelve or too elderly to stand are in the pews. The celebrant recites the prayers in a monotone, and the congregation responds with the singsong of rote. There is no music, no singing. The two readings are done by a priest, attired in his black suit and Roman collar, who uses no expression as he reads. The Gospel is read quickly. The homily consists of reading a mission fundraising letter from the bishop with a few comments by the priest on how the people should contribute so they might help export their deep sense of religion to other parts of the world. There is no handshake of peace. Two sisters assist in distributing the hosts (there is no wine offered) to the fifty percent of the congregation who approach the altar for communion. A Memorare is said after communion. The priest exits directly to the sacristy, and the members of the congregation chat as they leave for home.

The Eucharist

At dinner that evening, a local Protestant asks a tourist how the service was. She tells the visitor not to judge the whole country by that Mass. That particular parish has a reputation for poor liturgies. Still, the tourist knows that most of the congregation members were locals who continue to come despite the poor liturgies. The Eucharist undoubtedly holds some attraction for them.

Finally, a relatively new parish in an old church in Chicago celebrates the Eucharist in a way that attracts people from all over the Chicago area. In the five years that the attendance at a Sunday Mass has grown from fifteen people to over three hundred, a liturgy committee has tried to implement the new Mass in a way that addresses the needs and concerns of the congregation. Like most parishes, they have struggled with finding articulate readers, good musicians and music, and a sufficient number of eucharistic ministers. As the membership has grown from four people to over eight hundred, there are a variety of experiences to be considered when trying to correlate faith and life in a eucharistic celebration. In addition, the challenge to unity within the community and to service to the world beyond the community is not as easily met in a congregation that is not geographically centered.

The church, built in the 1850s, does not meet the design standards of most liturgical architects. Still, the people who gather there for Sunday liturgies find that the atmosphere of stained-glass windows and numerous statues stirs their religious imaginations in a way that the more sterile places designed by art and environment committees do not.

Mary G. Durkin

While the structures of pews and aisle in the old church do not seem conducive to a sense of being at a family meal, the friendliness of the people, the honest attempts to relate faith and life, the excellent homilies, and the many opportunities to participate in service activities help cement a sense of community among the members. The Lord made present in the Eucharist continues to be present in the interactions of the members in other activities.

In all three places, the liturgies, though quite different, follow the directions of the Order of the Mass. Yet, once the idea of Eucharist as a sacramental action of all those present is the criterion, the Order of the Mass will not automatically lead to eucharistic worship that is an effective symbol of the core of the Catholic faith. Each eucharistic community must be aware of the reason for their gathering together and continually work toward developing an atmosphere in their liturgies which makes them able to celebrate the memory of the Lord.

While these three official celebrations of the Eucharist were taking place, two unofficial liturgies were being held in the Chicago area. In a suburban community, people assembled for a Tridentine Mass offered by a recently ordained priest of the Society of St. Pius X. In a downtown highrise apartment building, a group of women gathered to "celebrate Eucharist" without the presence of an ordained priest. The first celebration represented a rejection of the new Order of the Mass as contrary to the basic beliefs of the faith. The second celebration found the Order of the Mass inadequate because the Church limits the role of priest to the male members of the community.

The Eucharist

Prior to the Council, neither group would have thought it possible to question Rome. Now, from different perspectives, both groups challenge Roman directives. The Society of St. Pius X wants a return to the system of the late Middle Ages. The women, claiming precedent in the apostolic communities, want the Church to move beyond its male orientation in selecting priests.

These five eucharistic celebrations are only examples of how, in practice, the Eucharist after the Council has variety in styles. Some African liturgies have added African cultural elements to the Roman liturgy while, in a few instances, specific African rites have been approved and African eucharistic prayers have been proposed. In Latin America, the basic Christian communities (*Comunidades de Base*) celebrate Eucharists geared to strengthening them as they struggle against injustice.

Even in those instances when the celebrations have Church approval, there are various interpretations as to how to implement the official directives, including many unofficial additions or subtractions from the formal structure. Every Mass is no longer the same.

In summary, as a result of the radical changes initiated by the Second Vatican Council, both eucharistic practices and eucharistic interpretations have moved in directions never imagined by most Catholics prior to the Council. One fact that seems obvious to a contemporary Catholic twenty-five years after the Council is that the Eucharist has many layers of meaning. Some of these layers are being explored theologically and liturgically by the *magisterium* and by the general membership of the Church. As is prob-

Mary G. Durkin

ably true of every religious symbol, the core symbol of the Catholic sacramental system continues to challenge each generation to search anew for its meaning. As the search continues, the searchers have the chance to discover how Christ's command to remember continues to be a challenge for all.

CHAPTER SEVEN

The Eucharist: 2013

WHEN Catholics at the end of the twentieth century celebrate the Eucharist, their "remembrance of me" ritual is vastly different from the ritual their religious forbears celebrated at the end of the nineteenth century. Underlying this difference is the contemporary emphasis on relating faith to the world in which Catholics live that faith. The Eucharist, the core expression of meaning for the Catholic community, seeks to make the absent one present in the world while at the same time that community waits for the day when "Christ will come again."

While there has been upheaval associated with the changed perceptions of the meaning of being a Catholic and the meaning of the Eucharist that followed the Second Vatican Council, there also has been a growing appreciation for how faith answers the meaning questions of the modern world. At the same time, the emphasis on Eucharist that calls for participation and commitment from all the faithful has helped underscore the importance of experience as a source of God's revelation. Correlating faith and experience and thereby enriching both has been a definite plus for this period.

Mary G. Durkin

The twenty-five-plus years since the *Constitution of the Liturgy* first appeared have been filled with new insights in the various layers of meaning contained in the rich symbol of the Eucharist. Church authorities, theologians, liturgists, pastoral workers, and the contemporary Catholic in the pew all feel the effects of these new insights.

Unlike the time after the Council of Trent, these twenty-five years have seen ongoing change in eucharistic interpretation and practice. Many contemporary Catholics wonder how long this change will continue. Some of those who wonder look forward to a time when there will be a stability similar to what existed before the Council. Others worry that the explorations of the rich symbolism of the Eucharist will be curtailed by those who see change as threatening to basic beliefs.

Predictions about the future are always difficult. In a time of conflicting opinions about what the future should look like, the crystal ball of one who tries to predict is quite cloudy. The contemporary Catholic, however, can hypothesize about what the state of eucharistic practice and interpretation might look like in 2013, fifty years after the framing of the *Constitution on the Liturgy*. Certain trends in the work of the *magisterium,* of theologians, and of liturgists suggest which issues will still be under discussion for years to come. Also, many of the leaders interpreting the meaning of the Eucharist and directing liturgical practices today will continue to be influential twenty or more years from now.

However, just as there is uncertainty about the directions in which the Church will move in the next twenty-five

The Eucharist

years, there also is no clear vision of what society will be like in the second decade of the twenty-first century. As this study has shown, the world in which the Church finds itself also plays a role in the direction the Church moves and the way the Eucharist reflects that movement. A contemporary Catholic, familiar with the ideas explored in the previous chapters, is safer simply making suggestions for what those involved in framing the future of the Eucharist could do. Given the importance of symbolic religious actions in the search for meaning, every contemporary Catholic has a stake in how the Catholic community interprets and practices its core sacrament. The suggestions that a contemporary Catholic makes can reflect his or her hopes for how eucharistic theory and practice will evolve.

Predictions

In light of the present bent of the teaching authority of the Church and of episcopal appointments in the 1980s, it appears that the *magisterium's* stance of caution about innovations beyond those in the 1969 Order of the Mass will continue. This stance could well include the refusal to reconsider the current theological arguments it uses against the ordination of women. As a result, more women will turn to nonofficial celebrations of the Eucharist. The percentage of women who do this will, however, remains small.

Nevertheless, if the shortage of priests continues the Church will be forced either to limit the availability of eu-

Mary G. Durkin

charistic celebrations or to tap some other source of presiders over the Eucharist. For these reasons, it seems that the Church will continue to need to focus on the theology of the priesthood and its relationship to the Eucharist.

Given the long history of emphasis on the Eucharist as the Real Presence, Sacrifice of the Mass, and source of unity, it seems that theologians and the *magisterium* will continue to explore the meaning of those terms. So, too, the understanding of the Eucharist as the core sacrament and as a mystery of faith will be investigated using the insights into symbol in human communication.

Given the continuing presence of poverty and of unrest in the world and in all human institutions, including the Church, St. Paul's command to the Corinthians will still be a valid reminder for those who participate in the Eucharist. They will be expected to follow Christ's example of care and concern for all who suffer any oppression.

Ecumenical discussions will be ongoing. Those who engage in this dialogue will likely have a deepening sense that unity of the Christian churches is a possibility. However, given the present bent of the *magisterium,* there will not be official approval of shared communion between Catholics and other churches. Despite this position, the practice probably will be more widespread in local eucharistic celebrations than it is in the 1980s.

Liturgists will continue to explore ways of developing liturgies that make the absent one present to the variety of human experiences of the world of 2013. Depending on their willingness to listen to those experiences and not act out of preconceived ideas, they will be successful. If the lit-

The Eucharist

urgists do not respond to their experiences, individual groups will design their own eucharistic celebrations. Out of desperation, some communities will disband all art and environment committees, music committees, and liturgical committees. In place of these committees they will select members of the communities with talents in these areas to learn the art of correlating faith, art, and life.

The laity in 2013 will be as diverse as they are in the 1980s. Some will want greater participation in liturgical celebrations that are designed to make Christ present in their midst. Others will be content with liturgies like those in the resort town of Ireland. Still others who have no options other than poor liturgies will turn to other sources for inspiration.

All in all, these predictions reflect an uneasiness about how the Church will proceed over the next twenty-five years. There is a possibility that those authorities who want conformity will succeed. In that case, their attempts to halt any development in eucharistic practice and interpretation will lead to a stress-filled Church.

Suggestions

A contemporary Catholic who has made a study of the Eucharist is in a position to offer some suggestions to those who are responsible for the future of the Eucharist. In the immediate future and continuing on into the next century, the *magisterium,* theologians, liturgists, and the laity all need to be attentive to what they can do to help explore the

Mary G. Durkin

richness of the eucharistic symbol. The following suggestions to each of these groups are guidelines that could help avert a sense of crisis in 2013.

The Magisterium—1) Those in positions of authority in the Church must be more trusting of the experiences of all the faithful. The fear of scandalizing the faithful is a carry-over from an earlier era, and, in fact, is insulting.

2) The whole issue of priesthood needs examination. This examination will be more effective if it includes listening to the experience of priesthood as it is lived out by priests and perceived by the laity. Alternatives to the present life-long commitment to celibacy could be explored.

3) The issue of the ordination of women must be opened for serious investigation and discussion. In a world where women's role is rapidly changing, even in those countries that are not as developed as Europe and the United States, the refusal to even discuss the issues makes it more and more difficult for the Eucharist to be a sign of unity.

4) Ecumenical discussions should continue but will be more effective if coupled with an openness to sharing in the communion of other Churches. More encouragement of ecumenical interaction at the local level could be encouraged.

5) Some regulation of liturgy might be necessary for the unity of a worldwide Church. However, an attitude that suggests guidelines rather than one that issues laws and censures those who are reported as deviating from the laws would help create a greater sense of unity.

The Eucharist

6) Statements from Rome could use language that does not need extensive interpretation in order to be understood by the average priest or lay person. In an era of mass media, those responsible for quick summaries of Roman pronouncements are not skilled in interpreting the nuances that permeate most papal statements.

Theologians—1) Catholic theologians trying to interpret the Eucharist in a way that is meaningful for the modern world must be in continual dialogue with other human disciplines. The insights into human experience gained in this dialogue provide material for theological reflections that can enrich both human experience and understanding of faith.

2) Theological discourse has its own language and its own issues. Often both the language and the issues are of little interest to the rest of the faith community. Yet, the insights gained in theological investigation often can be presented to the theologically untrained in less technical language.

3) While academic theology will always be a necessary discipline, the Catholic community also needs pastoral theologians. Pastoral theologians are those who identify concrete issues in human experience that continually raise new questions for theological reflection. Trained pastoral theologians are skilled artists who know how to listen to what is going on in a community and identify meaningful questions even before they have been formulated. The pastoral theologian then tries to help the community articulate

Mary G. Durkin

the question and search for its religious meaning. Eucharistic celebrations are places where these meaningful questions can be surfaced.

Priest—1) The priest and the Eucharist are intrinsically linked in the Catholic tradition. If, as Pope John Paul II maintains, priests are only worth what their eucharistic lives are worth, performing their role in the Eucharist well ought to be the primary goal of all priests. Though they now celebrate the Eucharist *with* the congregation instead of *for* the congregation, they still play a crucial role in gathering the eucharistic community as it acts in Christ's memory.

2) Priests must see their role as pastoral leaders and presiders at the Eucharist as one requiring artistic skill. They are on the front line as pastoral theologians. As such, they must become skilled listeners so their eucharistic celebrations respond to the needs of the community. They need to "see" the situations in their community and present the issues in a way that will help others see, too.

3) Homilies are a critical indicator of a priest's eucharistic worth. Failure to prepare homilies that invite the community to a deeper understanding of how they celebrate the Eucharist in Christ's memory and take his presence with them in their lives is a serious defect in a priest's eucharistic life. In preparing a homily a priest should bear in mind that making one good point a week adds up to fifty-two suggestions for how to "remember" Christ over the course of a year. It is not the length of the homily that counts.

The Eucharist

4) As the presiders at the eucharistic celebrations, priests also have a responsibility to encourage the community to find ways to be of service to the world in which they live and work. Priests ought to be active pastoral leaders, creating an environment in which the community members can reflect on their responsibilities and devise ways to fulfill them.

Liturgists—1) Liturgists, lay and clerical, must be artists in the sense that they need creative imaginations that call forth appreciation for the experiences of those who participate in the liturgy. Though an artist has a natural talent, this talent benefits from immersion in good artistic experiences. Liturgists need to acquire the same skills that are required of pastoral theologians. They must learn to listen to the people in the community they serve, uncovering those experiences that look to the Eucharist for a sense of meaning.

2) The primary guideline for eucharistic practices cannot be "if it was used in the early Church, it should be used now." The sense of earlier eucharistic rituals ought to be present but specific practices that were meaningful then are not necessarily able to evoke that same sense at a later time in a different culture. Some rituals from previous eras have universal meaning and can contribute a sense of continuity and unity to the Eucharist. Learning to determine what evokes a response in the community requires paying attention to the community.

3) It is important to encourage widespread participation in the Eucharist through the use of readers, choir, cantors,

Mary G. Durkin

ushers, greeters and servers. However, those who assume these roles need encouragement to view them as making an important contribution to the celebration. A participatory ritual requires that all who participate perform their roles well. Not every member of the community has the skills necessary to perform these roles in a way that does not detract from the flow of the celebration. If volunteers do not succeed in these roles, those responsible for the liturgy might consider hiring and/or training people who will make a commitment to their role.

4) Liturgical music is not performance music, and choirs, cantors, and leaders of song ought not to be performers. When the music at a eucharistic celebration is planned as part of the overall liturgy, it opens another avenue for experiencing God's presence. One style of music does not need to be preferred over another as long as the music used is good and enhances the liturgy. If the congregation is to join in singing, the songs ought to be ones they can sing.

5) Longer is not necessarily better. There are physical and probably psychological limits to how long people can be attentive to the ritual. Thirty-second or one minute pauses at pre-determined times generally are long enough to be annoying and not long enough for serious reflection. Members of the congregation ought to have the freedom to reflect at their own leisure.

6) The environment of the Church needs to be conducive to the sense of the Eucharist. This, however, does not mean creating all-purpose sterile buildings. Also art and environment committees that attempt to remove marble al-

The Eucharist

tars and altar rails and place the altar on the level of the congregation might be trying to imitate early Christian eucharistic gatherings. However, the modern Sunday congregation might not view the altar rail as an obstacle to participation while people in the back of the church might find an inability to witness the actions of the celebrant an unwelcome challenge. Remodelling of churches and design of new churches should be geared to the religious sensibilities and needs of the present congregations.

7) Liturgists ought to be in the forefront of an attempt to encourage *good* contemporary religious art. Through the ages, good religious art has been sacramental, reminding those who experience it of God's presence.

Laity—1) Lay people need to recognize their integral role in the celebrating community and the responsibility that is part of that role. Hans Küng once suggested three reasons why Sunday worship was important. First of all, the individual needs the weekly reminder of how faith and life are in constant conversation. Catholics are a people of community. The Catholic tradition has always been that of finding God in the midst of community. Secondly, the community needs individuals to come together on a weekly basis as a way of supporting each other in their faith commitment. Lastly, the society-at-large needs a continuous making-present of the absent one to the world. The symbolic impact of the Catholic Sunday liturgy impacts on the world outside the community.

2) Lay people ought to feel responsible for the quality of the liturgy both by the quality of their participation and by

Mary G. Durkin

their demand for liturgies that make the absent one present to them and their world.

3) Lay people must search for ways they can carry the presence of Christ found in the Eucharist into the world beyond the eucharistic celebration. The old Catholic Action ditty is still appropriate, though it requires some modification in language: "Mr. Business went to Church; he never missed a Sunday. Mr. Business went to hell for what he did on Monday."

In conclusion, the contemporary Catholic should keep in mind three thoughts that are obvious from this study of the Eucharist. First of all, the eucharistic ritual that owes its beginnings to a fellowship meal Christ celebrated with his disciples prior to his Passion and death has developed different styles throughout the history of Christianity. Its symbolic power as the core sacrament of the Catholic sacramental system has, at times, been muted by overadaptation to cultural practices. However, even during those periods when it seemed farthest removed from the original fellowship meal, segments of the Catholic community continued to live lives that remembered the command of Christ.

Secondly, the power of Christ's presence in a eucharistic celebration is a gift from God that can be experienced despite human actions that seem to block the making present of the absent one. The predictions of a contemporary Catholic might not come to fruition. The suggestions might be ignored. Still, the lesson of this study of the Eucharist suggests that the ebb and flow of the Church in its ability to be the body of Christ is reflected in the ebb and flow of an appreciation for the Eucharist as the continuous

The Eucharist

making-present of Christ to the world. Human limitations will always affect the way the Eucharist is able to express the meaning of life. The promise of Christ, however, is that the Spirit will use human experience to challenge the Church to move beyond human limitations.

Finally, the historical record shows that the Spirit has intervened numerous times to challenge the Church to renewal. The most recent intervention was in the person of Pope John XXIII and the Second Vatican Council. Undoubtedly, a Third Vatican Council will be needed at some point in the future. If the Eucharist in 2013 seems to once again be the victim of stagnation, the contemporary Catholic at that time will be in a position to call for a renewal.

READING LIST

Bausch, William J., *A New Look At the Sacraments* (Mystic, Connecticut: Twenty-Third Publications, 1983).

Bernier, Paul J. (ed.), *Bread from Heaven: Essays on the Eucharist* (New York: Paulist Press, 1977).

_____, *Bread Broken and Shaped* (Notre Dame, Indiana: Ave Maria Press, 1981).

Bouyer, Louis, *Eucharist: Theology and Spirituality of the Eucharistic Prayer* (Notre Dame: University of Notre Dame Press, 1968).

Cooke, Bernard, *Sacraments & Sacramentality* (Mystic, Connecticut: Twenty-Third Publications, 1983).

Cunningham, Lawrence S., *The Catholic Faith: An Introduction* (Mahwah, N.J.: Paulist Press, 1987).

David, J.G. (ed.), *The New Westminster Dictionary of Liturgy and Worship* (Philadelphia: The Westminster Press, 1986).

Deiss, Lucien, *It's the Lord's Supper: Eucharist of Christians* (New York: Paulist Press, 1976).

_____, *Springtime of the Liturgy* (Collegeville, Minnesota: The Liturgical Press, 1979).

Downey, Michael, *Clothed in Christ: The Sacraments and Christian Living* (New York: Crossroad, 1987).

Mary G. Durkin

Durkin, M.G. & Greeley, A.M. *How to Save the Catholic Church* (New York: Viking Press, 1984).

Eigo, Francis A. (ed.), *The Sacraments: God's Love and Mercy Actualized* (Villanova, Pennsylvania: The Villanova University Press, 1979).

Falconer, Alan D., "To Walk Together: The Lima Report on Baptism, Eucharist, Ministry." *Furrow* 34: 35-42 January, 1983.

Ganoczy, Alexandre, *An Introduction to Catholic Sacramental Theology* (New York: Paulist Press, 1984).

Guzie, Tad W., *Jesus and the Eucharist* (New York: Paulist Press, 1974).

Huels, John M., *One Table, Many Laws: Essays on Catholic Eucharistic Practice* (Collegeville, Minnesota: The Liturgical Press, 1986).

Kavanagh, Aidan, *Elements of Style: A Handbook of Liturgical Style* (New York: Pueblo Publishing Co., 1982).

Keifer, Ralph A., *Blessed and Broken: An Exploration of the Contemporary Experience of God in Eucharistic Celebration* (Wilmington, Delaware: Michael Glazier, Inc., 1983).

Kilmartin, Edward J., *Christian Liturgy: Theology and Practice* (Kansas City, Missouri: Sheed & Ward, 1988).

Lawler, Michael G., *Symbol and Sacrament: A Contemporary Sacramental Theology* (New York: Paulist Press, 1987).

Lee, Bernard (ed.), *Alternative Futures for Worship: The Eucharist* (Collegeville, Minnesota, 1987).

The Eucharist

Léon-Dufour, Xavier, *Sharing the Eucharistic Bread: The Witness of the New Testament* (New York: Paulist Press, 1987).

Martimort, A.G. (ed.), *The Church at Prayer: The Eucharist* (New York: Herder and Herder, 1973).

Martos, Joseph, *Doors to the Sacred: A Historical Introduction to Sacraments in the Catholic Church* (Garden City, New York: Image Books, 1982).

O'Carroll, Michael, *Corpus Christi: An Encyclopedia of the Eucharist* (Wilmington, Delaware: Michael Glazier, Inc., 1988).

Osborne, Kenan B., *Sacramental Theology: A General Introduction* (New York: Paulist Press, 1988).

Powers, David N., *The Sacrifice We Offer: The Tridentine Dogma and Its Reinterpretation* (New York: Crossroad, 1987).

Powers, Joseph M., *Eucharistic Theology* (New York: Herder and Herder, 1967).

Rahner, Karl & Haussling, Angelus, *The Celebration of the Eucharist* (New York: Herder & Herder, 1968).

Schillebeeckx, E., *Christ the Sacrament of the Encounter with God* (New York: Sheed and Ward, 1963).

_____, *The Eucharist* (New York: Sheed and Ward, 1968).

Thurian, Max, *The Mystery of the Eucharist: an Ecumenical Approach* (London: Mowbray, 1983).

_____, (ed.), *Ecumenical Perspectives on Baptism, Eucharist and Ministry* (Geneva: World Council of Churches, 1983).

QUESTIONS FOR DISCUSSION

1. How would you explain the difference between *The Baltimore Catechism*'s definition of sacrament and Michael Lawler's definition? What is the significance of this difference for a contemporary appreciation of sacraments? For a contemporary appreciation of the Eucharist?

2. What is the difference between a sign and a symbol? What are some examples of a sign? Of a symbol?

3. How do our religious symbols differ from other symbols?

4. Why does the Catholic sacramental system qualify as a symbolic system?

5. What are the biblical roots of the Catholic sacraments? How can the Church claim that Christ instituted the sacraments?

6. How would you summarize the development of the Catholic sacramental system from the Patristic period through the Council of Trent? What would be the main

Mary G. Durkin

points to remember in this historical development? Who are some of the critical thinkers to remember and why?

7. What would you say are the most important new understandings of sacrament as a result of Vatican II?

8. Why is the Eucharist the core sacrament of the Catholic system?

9. How do most of the people you know define the Eucharist?

10. Considering the New Testament accounts of the institution of the Eucharist, how would you answer the questions: a) What did Jesus do at the Last Supper? and b) What did Jesus mean by what he did?

11. What did the early Christians do when they gathered together? What did they mean by what they did?

12. What is the importance of the Jewish background out of which the Eucharist developed?

13. What were the critical concerns of the Patristic era and how might these have affected the way the Eucharist evolved during that time? What did this period add to eucharistic practices and interpretations?

14. What were some of the critical issues in the life and

The Eucharist

thought of the Middle Ages which influenced the development of the Eucharist during that long period?

15. What are the main differences between the eucharistic practices of the Middle Ages and those of earlier periods? Between eucharistic interpretation?

16. Why did the Reformers have a legitimate quarrel with the eucharistic practices of the late Middle Ages?

17. What are the main differences between the positions of the Reformers and those of Trent?

18. What would you consider the positive values of Trent's position on the Eucharist? What negative influences did it have?

19. What are the differences between the Tridentine Mass and the ritual meal of the New Testament?

20. How was the Second Vatican Council both the culmination of a century and a half of liturgical and theological study and also the impetus for even more study?

21. How have the changes in the Mass influenced the perception of what it means to be a Catholic?

22. What are some important features of the post-Vatican II eucharistic discussion? What are the effects of new interpretations of the meaning of the Eucharist?

Mary G. Durkin

23. What makes a "good" eucharistic celebration?

24. What do you see as some important challenges to eucharistic interpretations in the coming years?

25. How do you see the Eucharist functioning as the core symbol of the Catholic sacramental system in the twenty-first century?